STEPHEN BERESFORD

Stephen Beresford is a writer for stage and screen. He trained at RADA and his first play *The Last of the Haussmans* opened at the National Theatre, London, starring Julie Walters in 2012 to great critical and commercial success. His stage adaptation of Ingmar Bergman's *Fanny & Alexander* was first performed at The Old Vic, London, in 2018. His one-person play *Three Kings* was written for Andrew Scott to perform as part of *Old Vic: In Camera*, a series of live performances streamed from The Old Vic during the Covid-19 shutdown in 2020.

His first screenplay was *Pride* (2014), directed by Matthew Warchus. It premiered at Cannes Film Festival where it closed Directors' Fortnight. The film won three British Independent Film Awards (including Best British Film) and was nominated in four further categories, received the South Bank Show Award for Best British Film, and was nominated for BAFTA Best British Film, Golden Globe Best Motion Picture and London Critic's Circle British Film of the Year. Stephen won the BAFTA Award for Outstanding Debut.

Stephen Beresford

THE
SOUTHBURY
CHILD

NICK HERN BOOKS

London

www.nickhernbooks.co.uk

A Nick Hern Book

The Southbury Child first published in Great Britain in 2022 as a paperback original by Nick Hern Books Limited, The Glasshouse, 49a Goldhawk Road, London W12 8QP

The Southbury Child copyright © 2022 Stephen Beresford

Cover image: Alex Jennings in the original production of *The Southbury Child*, 2022; design by Muse Creative Communications

Designed and typeset by Nick Hern Books, London
Printed in the UK by Mimeo Ltd, Huntingdon, Cambridgeshire PE29 6XX

A CIP catalogue record for this book is available from the British Library

ISBN 978 1 84842 974 1

The Southbury Child was first co-produced by London Theatre
Company and Chichester Festival Theatre, and performed at
Chichester Festival Theatre on 17 June 2022, before
transferring to the Bridge Theatre, London, on 1 July. The cast
was as follows (in order of appearance):

DAVID HIGHLAND	Alex Jennings
LEE SOUTHBURY	Josh Finan
NAOMI HIGHLAND	Racheal Ofori
JANET ORAM	Hermione Gulliford
SUSANNAH HIGHLAND	Jo Herbert
MARY HIGHLAND	Phoebe Nicholls
CRAIG COLLIER	Jack Greenlees
JOY SAMPSON	Holly Atkins
TINA SOUTHBURY	Sarah Twomey

Director	Nicholas Hytner
Set Designer	Mark Thompson
Costume Designer	Yvonne Milnes
Lighting Designer	Max Narula
Sound Designer	George Dennis
Casting Director	Robert Sterne
Costume Supervisor	Rosemary Elliott-Dancs
Props Supervisor	Lily Mollgaard
Assistant Director	Isabel Marr
Production Manager	Chris Hay

For my mother, who first took me into a church

And for the gentleman at St Thomas the Apostle, Hollywood,
who unlocked the door again, forty-odd years later

8

Characters

DAVID HIGHLAND, *late fifties/early sixties, vicar of the Parish of St Saviour's, Dartmouth*
MARY HIGHLAND, *late fifties/early sixties, his wife*
NAOMI HIGHLAND, *early thirties, their (adopted) daughter*
SUSANNAH HIGHLAND, *mid-thirties, their daughter*
LEE SOUTHBURY, *late twenties/early thirties, uncle of Taylor Southbury*
TINA SOUTHBURY, *early thirties, mother of Taylor Southbury*
JOY SAMPSON, *thirties, police officer, pregnant*
CRAIG COLLIER, *late thirties, new curate*
JANET ORAM, *fifties, doctor's wife*

Note on the Text

Stage directions are intended for the reader, and not for the actor. Although it wouldn't do any harm for the actor to take a look too.

This text went to press before the end of rehearsals and so may differ slightly from the play as performed.

ACT ONE

1.

*Kitchen of the vicarage. Slightly Gothic, maybe – large,
anyway – a hangover from when this was a place of prestige.
The room is filled with more than just kitchenware – books, art,
piled-up ashtrays – and is dominated by a huge dining table,
loaded with paperwork, newspapers and magazines.* LEE
SOUTHBURY *sits, in his anorak, slumped in a seat at the
dining table.* DAVID HIGHLAND *is opposite him, examining
papers. A pot of tea and two mugs on the table. It's a brutal
night – wind outside, rain.*

DAVID *picks up a sheet of paper.*

DAVID. I christened you... You *and* your sister... Southbury...
Your father, wasn't he a Seale Arms man?

LEE. That's putting it mildly.

DAVID. He had a nickname –

LEE. Whizz.

DAVID. That's right. First time I encountered a christening party
before the service. Paralytic, we were. I'm ashamed to say,
I had to be guided through the whole thing by my verger –
Virtually pointed me at the font. The redoubtable Mrs Irene
Hammond. Scourge of the Sea Cadets. Much missed.

Silence. DAVID *smiles, kindly.*

And now we are here.

LEE *nods. Looks down. Quite a long silence.*

There was a time when we all thought... When we all very
much believed that Taylor had turned the corner... I remember
the collection for Disneyland. We had a service here.
Blessings and prayers – And there was a search, wasn't
there? For a donor?

LEE. She got bad again very quick. They were back in hospital on the Monday, then –

DAVID. Is that usual?

LEE. I'm sorry?

DAVID. With the disease. The speed, I mean –

LEE. When you're little. When you're Taylor's age... When you're older it can take a longer time to work through the body. That's what they told us. But when you're a little kid –

DAVID. I understand.

He makes a note.

By the way – I've been meaning to ask you – Taylor's father.

LEE. What about him?

DAVID. Should I mention him?

LEE. If you do, you'll be the only fucker who knows who he was. Pardon me. My sister's the only one who knows, and she's not telling.

DAVID *nods, scribbles a note.*

DAVID. We'll leave him out of it, then.

LEE. I was more of a father to her than anyone else –

DAVID. Of course.

LEE. Father *and* uncle. Only stable figure in her life. Probably.

DAVID *nods. Sure. Back to the diary.*

DAVID. Shall we talk about dates? The dreaded river blessing is, of course, next Saturday.

LEE (*quietly*). Fucking grockles.

DAVID. And – Yes – Since we don't want to have the hearse involved in a three-mile tailback... I'm going to suggest the beginning of the following week. The seventeenth for example. That's a Tuesday. Ten a.m.? I think that's best. That way you don't have to... I think it's the waiting that's hard. Waiting around all day for it to start.

DAVID *looks up.* LEE *isn't making notes.*

We will, I'm afraid, have to talk about one aspect of the service – as suggested by your sister. It's just one small thing, but I would like to explain it to you. If I may. Why I feel that it's perhaps not the best idea.

LEE. Do you ever think... I don't know –

DAVID. What?

LEE. I don't know. It's a funny job, isn't it? Yours. I'm not being rude.

DAVID. It is, yes. That's a very accurate description. And I don't think it's rude at all.

LEE. I'm not... anything.

DAVID. Right.

LEE. That's not to say – You know – I'm just – I'm not religious.

DAVID. That's perfectly okay. I am.

DAVID *smiles.* LEE *doesn't. He nods.*

LEE. That's funny.

DAVID. What do you do, Lee?

LEE. Nothing.

DAVID. Nothing?

LEE. I was a carpenter. Sand Quay.

DAVID. Ah.

LEE. They laid us all off.

DAVID. And how are you getting on with all this?

LEE. I'm fine.

DAVID. It's a very hard task you've been given.

LEE. I'm fine. Honestly.

DAVID. We can go as slowly or as briskly as you like.

LEE. I'm fine. Briskly. Or slowly. It makes no odds to me. I'm fine.

A little silence.

DAVID. Tina has no particular preference when it comes to hymns. Your mother has asked for 'All Things Bright and Beautiful', which, of course... And for a couple of pieces of secular music – both of which are fine –

LEE. They don't want –

DAVID. Yes?

LEE. I don't know if they said anything –

DAVID. Go on –

LEE. They don't want it to be – too – 'Funeral'. They want it to be a celebration of her life.

Beat.

DAVID. Lee, your sister has asked about some balloons – about tying some helium balloons to the pews and the altar –

LEE. She doesn't want it to be like church... She wants it to be more – Taylor loved cartoons, and all that – Disneyland. The Disney princesses –

DAVID. Yes –

LEE. She thinks that's what she would have wanted.

DAVID. Yes. I understand that Taylor loved Disney. I did myself, as a child. My daughters did.

LEE. Make it less scary.

DAVID. Yes. I want to suggest something, Lee – I hope I can make myself clear. I don't think it's a good idea to hide the church behind balloons. I hope you understand what I mean by that.

LEE. It's just a bit more – For a little kid –

DAVID. When was the last time you were in the church?

LEE. I don't know –

DAVID. Don't worry, that's not a test.

LEE. School or something. Wedding. My little sister's wedding.

DAVID. You see, the church is already decorated, Lee. Beautifully decorated. 'Decorated in exuberant local style' if you'll forgive the breathless prose of *One Hundred Devon Churches*... Decorated with a very specific and sacred purpose – by men just like you. Men born in the town, and bred in it. Carpenters.

LEE. I bet they didn't get laid off with twenty-four hours' notice. Not so much as a meeting or a conversation.

DAVID. Indeed... (*Beat.*) I mean, I don't suppose the medieval bishops were the high watermark of industrial relations, but – Yes. Your point is taken. What I'm trying to say, is that the decoration in the church is there for a reason –

LEE. It's not about Disney.

DAVID. It's not. It's not about Disney. That's it, exactly.

LEE. No happy endings.

DAVID. No *easy* endings. No narrative closure. Magic, yes. Mystery – Of course – in abundance.

And the church can be brightened up. It needn't be sombre. Flowers – my wife will arrange flowers. Or you can arrange them yourself... That's – It's not about being gloomy... Are you sure you don't want any tea?

LEE. I thought you'd have something stronger.

DAVID. Ah... Yes... To tell you the truth I'm on a bit of a – I don't know if you heard about my little prang – ?

LEE. Up Jawbones?

DAVID. Yes –

LEE. It's a nasty bend.

DAVID. It is. It really, is.

LEE. Especially if you're pissed.

A little beat.

DAVID. Well, I've rather promised myself that I'm going to... Only for a week or two...

LEE. S'alright.

DAVID. I mean, obviously – that doesn't mean *you* can't. I just… I think if Mary came in –

LEE *gets up, walks around the room a bit.*

LEE. I suppose people are always coming in here, telling you things. 'Confess to their sins'?

DAVID. Well. Confession is a… (*Beat.*) Formalised confession is a Roman Catholic tradition, but…

LEE. What do they do? Kneel down?

DAVID. No.

LEE. 'Beg for forgiveness'?

DAVID. No. That's – No. They don't do that. They don't beg.

LEE. It's all Henry VIII, isn't it? Henry VIII wants to get his end away so we end up with a new religion. I mean – If he'd kept his cock in his trousers we'd all be Catholics. Wouldn't we?

DAVID. That's one way of looking at it, I suppose.

A little silence while LEE *examines the bookshelves.* DAVID *watches.*

LEE. Tights.

DAVID. Sorry?

LEE. Tights. Not trousers.

DAVID. Ah.

LEE. He would have worn tights.

DAVID. He would, yes.

LEE. He should have kept his cock in his tights.

DAVID. Yes. His codpiece. This conversation seems to have taken a rather independent turn –

LEE. I'm into history. I watch a lot of it. The thing about Henry VIII is – people forget – That was his nature. He couldn't help himself. They're like that –

DAVID. What?

LEE. Single-minded. Stubborn.

DAVID. The Tudors?

LEE. Gingers. Ginger-haired people… Do you know Mark Borden?

DAVID. I –

LEE. He works on the scaffolding. He's a ginger… He's a prick, actually. But – he's *focused*.

He picks up a photograph and shows it to DAVID. DAVID *smiles in acknowledgement.*

DAVID. Yes… Naomi… Do you know her?

LEE. I was at the primary with her.

DAVID. Of course.

LEE. She was… We were friends –

DAVID. Were you?

LEE. Kind of.

DAVID. I'll tell her I've seen you.

LEE. I'd say our lives have taken pretty different courses… She's back, in't she?

DAVID. Yes.

LEE. Couldn't handle it.

DAVID. Well…

LEE. I couldn't live in London. It's a fucking shithole.

DAVID. Have you been?

LEE. No. Still famous is she?

DAVID. Well – She's an actress.

LEE puts down the photograph.

The children of clergymen often seem to gravitate toward the stage. I'm not sure what that means exactly, but I have a feeling it doesn't reflect terribly well on us. The other route, of course, is teaching – That's what Susannah's done.

LEE. I could've been an actor.

Silence.

Or something.

DAVID. Lee –

LEE. You know this fucking place – this – Divine Light Mission?

DAVID. I – Yes. The Evangelicals?

LEE. They're in the school sports hall.

DAVID. So I believe.

LEE. They take it over once a week.

DAVID. Yes, that's – Yes.

LEE. My cousin was – She got all into it. They were doing it too. 'Prayers for Taylor.' 'Special Service.' We went there.

DAVID. Did you?

LEE. Packed hall. Packed. Kendra – my cousin – She'd go to anything, like – she's one of those twats who goes to the river blessing every year –

DAVID. When you say 'packed' –

LEE. I dunno –

DAVID. Fifty? Sixty?

LEE. Two hundred?

DAVID. *Two hundred?*

LEE. At least. Have you seen our shrine?

DAVID. Your – ?

LEE. Shrine. Outside the house. The shrine for Taylor.

DAVID. Oh – Yes. I've heard about it.

LEE. People started leaving stuff on the fence. Flowers and that. Candles. Makes a change from bags of dogshit I suppose...

Makes me laugh. They wouldn't spit on us before. Where were the fucking prayers when we were being evicted? When my mum was being investigated by Disability? The Southburys? Benefit fuckers. That child went to school two years running with no winter coat – they laughed at her, they treated her like filth. She gets sick and it's all – 'Oh – Sleep with the angels, little princess.' It makes me want to puke.

DAVID. Why don't you sit down, Lee?

LEE. I better – I'm going to go, actually. I'm –

He doesn't move.

Banging their drums and playing their guitars. Arms in the air. What are they, that lot? A rival church?

DAVID. They're – It's a small group of Evangelicals. He's a lay preacher – I've met him. It's not a church... Lee, what's the matter? What is all this? What's going on?

LEE *shakes his head.*

Does your mother really know you're here this evening? Does Tina?

LEE *shakes his head.*

You *weren't* sent here to finalise the arrangements, were you...?

Silence.

Lee – ?

LEE. When Taylor got sick again they sent us all to be tested. See if we were a match. I came back from the hospital and said that I was. But I wasn't.

Silence.

DAVID. ...Did you make a mistake?... It was a very stressful time... Often – in my experience – when people are receiving bad news – especially from a doctor – it can be confusing, overwhelming –

LEE. I didn't make a mistake. I knew what I was saying.

DAVID. Then, why?... How long did this go on for?

LEE. Couple days... I wanted it to be true. I... I wanted it. They think I did it to get free drinks and all that – to be patted on the back everywhere. But I wanted it to be true... And now... Tina won't speak. She won't speak to me. She hasn't said a word, since –

DAVID. How did they find out?

LEE. They rang the hospital. They said – 'What do we do now?' And they were like – 'He's made a mistake. He's not a match. We were very clear – He's not a match.'

DAVID. Lee, the nature of grief is such that it can make us behave in extraordinary ways. Rage, despair –

LEE. They always thought I was a fucking waste of space, anyway.

DAVID. Lee –

LEE (*distraught*). But – Why did I do it, though? Why?

DAVID. We're going to sort this out.

LEE. How? Tina won't speak to me. She won't even look at me.

DAVID. She's very angry – quite understandably –

LEE. But why? Why? Why did I do it?

DAVID. I'm going to call your mum right now –

LEE. No –

DAVID. I'm going to talk to her and I'm going to talk to Tina. Everything is going to be alright.

LEE (*quietly*). Oh, Jesus –

DAVID. Everything is going to be alright, Lee.

LEE. Jesus –

DAVID. Listen to me. Everything is going to be alright.

Black.

2.

*Early morning. Before 8 a.m. The curtains are drawn and the
light outside is pretty dim – growing, I suggest, through the
scene.* NAOMI HIGHLAND *is leaning against the kitchen
cabinet. She might be a little the worse for wear – and is
dressed in her clothes from the night before and so looks
incongruously glittery.*

*Leaning against the internal door – hovering as if reluctant to
come all the way in – is* JANET ORAM (*offstage wife of the
doctor in* The Last of the Haussmans). *She has the keys to her
car in her hands...* NAOMI *is hugging a cup of coffee as
though it might save her.*

JANET. Must be rather a strange feeling. Coming back to your
old home – your old room – especially after such a long time
away... The important thing, is not to consider it as some
kind of failure. A lot of people can't handle London... Peter
hated it. I loved it, of course – but then I was working in
finance so I was constantly stimulated.

NAOMI. That sounds nice.

JANET. I must say, you're very dressed up.

NAOMI. Oh, you know – Some mornings call for 'country
casual' – others... (*Looks down.*) Lithuanian prostitute.

JANET *'smiles'*.

JANET. I believe you were at Jeb Wintersham's party last night.

NAOMI. Who told you that?

JANET. Oh, I have my little spies... (*Quickly.*) Not Harry and
Fred – not my boys – they don't tell me anything. No – the
boy who does our boathouse, Paul – he was there. Said it
was quite the riot... I don't know what Diana Wintersham
will think – all that carousing in her lovely house. But I
suppose she wasn't there – They ski don't they?... Maybe
that's why you went! Make sure there was a grown-up
amongst all those young people. Do you know, this is
actually a lovely room...

She looks at her watch.

Are you planning on staying here?

NAOMI (*incredulous*). Here – ?

JANET. The town.

NAOMI. Jesus, no. It was bad enough when I was a child. No offence.

JANET (*stung*). I... None taken... To each his own... (*Recovering.*) The trick, of course, is to keep oneself terrifically busy. I'm always... Sailing, yacht club, regatta committee – Not to mention all the other duties of a country doctor's wife – *and* I've got a semi-derelict house to renovate... No, I don't miss London. Not a bit. And the natives are actually, quite – We've made a lot of friends. As long as you keep it light, and stay off 'the B-word'.

NAOMI. B-word?

JANET (*devoiced*). Brexit. Poor things – they have no idea what they've voted for. Honestly, my heart breaks – (*A gasp of inspiration.*) Pilates!

NAOMI. I'm sorry?

JANET. You could open a little Pilates studio! Now, that's something we're really crying out for – A little Pilates studio in the church hall. And I don't think you need much in the way of qualifications –

SUSANNAH HIGHLAND *appears at the door behind* JANET. *She is dressed for work – a plain skirt and top. A little dowdy.*

SUSANNAH. Mrs Oram – ?

JANET. Oh! Finally. I'm being denied entry –

NAOMI. I said she couldn't walk into matins.

SUSANNAH. You can't.

SUSANNAH*'s passed* JANET *now and is in the kitchen. She starts to make tea, perhaps.*

JANET. I just want to nip up the back path and slide into the church –

SUSANNAH. There's a religious service in progress.

JANET. I'll be like a little mouse.

SUSANNAH. I'm sorry, it's out of the question. Nobody uses the back door until the service is over.

NAOMI. Why can't you just go round the front and wait in the porch?

JANET. Because – as I've already explained to you, Naomi – I'm double-parked.

SUSANNAH. Our mother will be back in a minute – couldn't you talk to her?

JANET. It's your father I need – and it's very important. It's about Taylor Southbury's funeral.

SUSANNAH. Perhaps I could suggest you returned after matins.

JANET. Oh, come on, girls, let's be wild. Let's break the rules. I won't tell God, if you won't.

SUSANNAH. I expect Naomi offered you a cup of tea.

JANET (*stung*). Well, when your father gets in will you please tell him that I called?

SUSANNAH. Of course.

JANET. You might like to bear in mind that this is hardly the time for the vicar to be inaccessible. Just a thought.

JANET *leaves out through the house and to the front door.*
SUSANNAH *walks to the kitchen door to check that she's gone. We hear the sound of the front door closing.*
SUSANNAH *comes back.*

NAOMI. I've decided I'm going to be a coastguard.

SUSANNAH (*disbelief*). Have you only just got in?

NAOMI. Five minutes with Janet Oram and all ambition has drained from me.

SUSANNAH. Is that my belt?

NAOMI. Can I borrow it?

SUSANNAH. Where do you even find to go until – (*Looks at the clock*.) eight a.m.?

NAOMI. A party.

SUSANNAH. What party?

NAOMI. That Wintersham boy.

SUSANNAH. In South Town?

NAOMI. Positively stuffed with privileged brats. *Her* boys were there. They're actually alright, you know. The younger one – Fred is it – ? Is even kind of cute.

SUSANNAH. He's eighteen.

NAOMI. So what? He told me all about his ADHD, and his anxiety meds, and his new surfboard… Maybe that's where I got the idea for my career change…

SUSANNAH. You leave home to have an amazing life, Naomi – and that's fine – I accept that. But you can't come home and bring the amazing life with you. You can't live it under my nose.

NAOMI. There was a *lot* of talk about the vicarage. Took me back to the old days.

SUSANNAH. What talk?

NAOMI. 'Oh my God,' I thought – 'He's at it again…' Until I realised that Taylor Southbury *isn't*, in fact, one of his girlfriends –

SUSANNAH. Dear God – if I hear one more person's opinion about that funeral –

NAOMI. Yes, heaven forbid that the serfs should have something to say –

SUSANNAH. I doubt there were many serfs at Jeb Wintersham's.

NAOMI. They set up a speaker system on the tennis court – and they set off flares.

SUSANNAH. That's actually an offence. It confuses the coastguard... And anyway, Jeb Wintersham shouldn't be having a house party. Not with his parents away.

NAOMI. Yeah, cos we never went to an illegal rave, did we? Oh... well, you probably didn't – but I certainly did. And I'm glad the tradition carries on.

MARY HIGHLAND *enters. They stop.* MARY *immediately busies herself. It's her usual strategy upon entering any room.*

MARY. Naomi, why are you up?

NAOMI. I was shaken by an inner conviction that I should save lives.

MARY. Which lives?

NAOMI. The ones in peril on the sea.

MARY. Well, you'll have to save them elsewhere. Both of you. Our guest is arriving any minute.

NAOMI. Don't worry about me. I'm going straight back to bed.

SUSANNAH (*quietly*). I'm sorry, did you say 'back'?

MARY (*despairing*). Why is this phone never replaced on its nest?

SUSANNAH. It's nothing to do with me.

MARY. The battery drains if it's not replaced – How many times do I have to say it?

NAOMI. The doctor's wife was here.

MARY. What?

SUSANNAH. Janet Oram.

MARY. What did she want?

SUSANNAH. I expect you can guess.

NAOMI. Taylor Southbury.

MARY. Oh, for heaven's sake. Why on earth is she involving herself?

NAOMI. She's just the tip of the iceberg, from what I hear.

MARY. Naomi, if you're suddenly going to start getting up early, you might like to make yourself useful. Help your father at matins for example.

NAOMI. Do you know, I was literally halfway out the door – and then I remembered – I'm a militant atheist.

DAVID *enters. Main door.*

MARY. How was it?

DAVID. Cold. And sparsely attended. Clive Pearson, the two Miss Potters and Whispery Elizabeth.

MARY. Did anyone say anything?

DAVID. About what?

MARY. About Taylor Southbury's funeral.

DAVID. Difficult to say. I walked Whispery Elizabeth to her car. Trouble is – you never know whether you've just had a long speech or a long silence. (*Looks at phone.*) He's nearly here apparently.

NAOMI. 'The troubleshooter.'

MARY. He's not a troubleshooter – Stop calling him that.

SUSANNAH. What is he then?

DAVID. A slap on the wrist.

MARY (*to* DAVID). And don't you make light of it, either. (*To them.*) He's a curate. He's not senior to your father – in rank or experience. And he'll be taking a very junior role.

NAOMI. I don't understand why you don't just give her her sodding balloons.

MARY. Thank you. For the unsolicited viewpoint of the militant atheist.

SUSANNAH. Naomi's decided what she wants to do with her life, Dad.

DAVID. I was rather fond of the life she was leading.

NAOMI. I can't go on wearing stupid dresses and speaking words that aren't my own.

DAVID. Wretched child. You undermine the very basis of my existence.

MARY. Janet Oram was here.

DAVID. What?

MARY. I told you. I told you they would bring out the big guns.

DAVID. I welcome 'the big guns', whatever that means –

MARY. David –

DAVID. It's nothing to worry about.

A car pulling up outside. Everyone freezes slightly.

MARY. Out. Everyone.

DAVID. Is it him?

MARY. I think so.

NAOMI *goes toward the back door.*

NAOMI. I want to see him.

MARY. Go. Both of you. Susannah, you'll be late for school –

SUSANNAH. I'm going. I'm not in the least bit interested.

Both SUSANNAH *and* NAOMI *start to leave.*

MARY. And, Naomi, if you're going to have a bath, will you please not use all the hot water?

NAOMI. Why? Are you going to baptise him?

MARY. Go. Both of you. Now.

NAOMI. This is like a Jane Austen. 'A new curate for the parish! How giddy we've all become!'

MARY. Naomi –

NAOMI. 'Fear not, Mama. He will discover me at my cross-stitch hoop…'

She leaves.

MARY *goes back to looking through the glass of the back door. She turns back to* DAVID.

MARY. Janet Oram is *not* nothing.

DAVID. I know.

MARY. It's serious. And I want it stopped before it gets out of control.

She returns to the glass. The engine has stopped now.

Oh God. Look at his car.

DAVID. I like the tinted windows. Makes him look like a drug dealer.

MARY. Rather an unfortunate first impression, don't you think, for an ordained minister?

DAVID. Perhaps he is a drug dealer. Mary, I want you to answer me with absolute candour – Are you back on the smack?

Outside – car door closing, the beep of an auto-lock. MARY *steps back from the window.*

MARY. He's coming –

DAVID. How should I be?

MARY. If I thought it were possible, I'd ask you to be polite. I'll settle for uncontroversial. And, David – ? No jokes.

DAVID *takes a moment, throws open the back door, calls out.*

DAVID. 'Are you he whom we seek or must we wait for another?'

MARY. What did I just say?

DAVID. That's not a joke. It's John the Baptist. (*Shouting, off.*) I'm forbidden to be anything other than polite so I'll just point out that you're an hour and twenty minutes late and you have a pimp's car. Hello.

CRAIG COLLIER *arrives. Takes* DAVID*'s handshake as he comes in. He is forties, Scottish, good looking.*

CRAIG. Hello.

DAVID. I'm David Highland.

CRAIG. Craig. I'm so sorry – Somebody told me to take the
ferry – They said that the best way to see the town was from
the river –

DAVID. And so it is.

CRAIG. But then – The hills are very steep, aren't they? And
then I got lost – I was driving around for ages.

DAVID. And the car?

CRAIG. The car.

DAVID. The *car* – the tinted windows. The vulgarity of which
has shocked my wife into silence. I can't imagine what the
parishioners will think – they're used to having their spiritual
needs met in a Toyota Yaris.

MARY. Until you wrapped it round a lamp post.

DAVID. Until I wrapped it round a lamp post – there now – my
wife has spoken. And in her oblique, patrician manner she
has offered you an alliance – I suggest you seize it.

CRAIG. Hello –

MARY. Mary Highland.

CRAIG. Craig. Hi. I really am sorry.

MARY. You're here now.

CRAIG. I am. And I'm very glad to be. And – (*Exhales*.) Wow.
I didn't realise how serious things had got.

DAVID. Serious – ?

CRAIG. The level of hostility. I mean – I understand from the
diocese that your policy is to ride it out – and I can see that
you're doing just that – (*Gestures vaguely behind him*.) But –
If you'll allow me to say so, that's a very risky strategy. Not
just for you, but for the Church as a whole.

DAVID. Goodness. Straight into it.

CRAIG. I see no reason to delay. Especially with things at such
a head.

MARY. Perhaps we could settle you in a bit first –

A little awkward beat.

DAVID. Just look at this luggage, Mary –

MARY. I'm looking.

DAVID. We should have boys in white tunics to transport it up the stairs.

CRAIG. My partner has – Sorry. It's a perk of the job.

DAVID. In luggage?

CRAIG. In branding. I'm ashamed to say there's two more in the car.

DAVID. Oh – let me help you.

CRAIG. Certainly not –

MARY. For God's sake, David, watch your shoulder.

CRAIG. Stay where you are. Please. It's nothing – really. It'll only take me a second. Thank you.

He goes. They stare after him for a moment. DAVID *looks back at* MARY.

DAVID. What?

MARY 'Boys in white tunics.'

DAVID. Oh for God's sake –

MARY. He might be sensitive.

DAVID. About what – his sexuality? He mentioned his partner.

MARY. That doesn't mean it's open season.

DAVID. I'm trying to be light-hearted.

MARY. I think, of all the things that could be levelled against you –

DAVID. I'm not a bigot, Mary.

MARY. So why appear like one?

DAVID. I'm not a cannibal either – Jesus – what other things, that I'm *not* – should I *not* appear to be? A Maori? A backing vocalist? (*Looking through the door.*) He's got a tennis racket.

CRAIG *returns with some more bags.*

CRAIG. Your last curate left –

DAVID. Four years ago.

MARY. There are eight churches in this parish – and they are not close together. It really is a burden.

DAVID. This is a town of two parts. Shall I start the tour?

MARY. Let him unpack.

CRAIG. No. Really –

DAVID. The rich live here – (*Gestures.*) facing the water. Their summer houses and yachts were the view you enjoyed from the ferry. Second homes on the whole – and very grand, some of them – Londoners, chiefly. The local term of abuse is 'grockle'.

CRAIG. 'Grockle.' I like that.

DAVID. Good. Because that's what they'll call you. Then, at the other end, without a river view, we have the rest. The majority. They were once the fishing fleet, the shipwrights, the sailors –

CRAIG. Are they churchgoing – ? The – others, I mean – The majority?

DAVID. High days and holidays.

CRAIG. You said they used to be fishermen –

DAVID. Yes. And shipbuilders, until our yards were all shut down and turned into ceramics galleries.

CRAIG. So – now?

DAVID. They work in call centres. They clean the homes of the weekenders. They claim benefits.

MARY. Not all of them.

DAVID. I'm painting a picture.

MARY. Yes, a vivid one. And – if I may say so – somewhat partial.

DAVID. Mary grew up here. She has an investment in its reputation.

CRAIG. You grew up here?

DAVID. A noble family of wool merchants who started stealing land some time in the fourteenth century –

MARY. Craig, wouldn't you like to freshen up.

DAVID. You're never far from the medieval in this place. We even bless the river once a year, in a solemn and completely impenetrable ceremony...

CRAIG. And you – ?

DAVID. Oh, I'm a yob. My father worked for a carpet manufacturer, my mother was a dinner lady. 'Vicars in the Church of England can be socially mobile – but their spouses may not.' I expect they taught you that at Mirfield –

CRAIG. No.

MARY. Of course they didn't. It's errant nonsense. (*To* DAVID.) I don't know why you need to paint yourself in this way.

DAVID. In what way?

MARY. As a wry, classless observer –

DAVID. He asked for the tour.

MARY. But not from Louis Theroux.

DAVID. Listen – you mustn't worry too much about this Southbury business. I know what they told you – And it *is* delicate – of course it is – but really – the whole thing has been somewhat overstated.

MARY. What are you talking about?

DAVID. I don't mean them – I don't mean the family. They're the only people in all this who have my respect and my sympathy.

No, I mean the reaction in the town. I promise you – half of them don't even know what they're protesting about.

CRAIG. That really isn't my impression, David.

DAVID *is a little taken aback by this forthright statement.*

DAVID. Oh? And what's your impression, Craig?

CRAIG. One of tremendous hostility, David. One that needs to be taken very seriously.

MARY. Hear, hear.

DAVID. And this is based on the five minutes you've spent here, is it?

CRAIG (*gestures behind again*). Five very instructive minutes, yes.

SUSANNAH *appears at the inside door.*

DAVID. This is Susannah. My eldest. Make friends. She's a pillar of the primary school, a verger of the church –

SUSANNAH. Hello.

DAVID. Quite indispensable. I've done my best to crush her spirit so she never leaves.

SUSANNAH. Mission accomplished. Has anyone seen my guitar?

MARY. You're going to be late.

SUSANNAH. I know that. Thank you.

DAVID *goes for* CRAIG's *bags.*

DAVID. Come on. Let's make a tour of inspection –

CRAIG. Please – let me at least help you.

DAVID. No, no – I'll fling these onto the bed, and we can tour the kingdom. Who knows – we might even stop for a stiffener at The Seven Stars.

CRAIG. I don't drink. Sorry.

DAVID. What?

CRAIG. I don't drink. I don't drink alcohol.

DAVID. What never?

CRAIG. Never.

DAVID. Not even a shandy?

CRAIG. I categorically and absolutely never touch alcohol, David. And I don't know why I said I was sorry just now – because I'm not. I'm not sorry.

Little silence.

MARY. Susannah, shouldn't you be going?

SUSANNAH. I've got five minutes.

DAVID. Well… Never mind. A Franciscan of my acquaintance used to preach on the subject of hard liquor. Specifically, the treatment of hangovers in the Old Testament.

CRAIG. I don't –

DAVID. 'Moses took two tablets.' (*Declaiming, suddenly.*) 'This is *he*, of whom it is written, Behold, I send my messenger before thy face – !'

He's gone. SUSANNAH *regards* CRAIG *for a moment before she goes back into the hall.*

MARY. Calvinism? Or something else?

CRAIG. I'm sorry?

MARY. The drinking. You don't have to answer.

CRAIG. It's something else.

MARY. I must say I admire the archdeacon's sense of humour.

CRAIG. I don't think it's intentional.

MARY. Don't you? (*Beat.*) I'm aware of what you think you see here.

CRAIG. That's rather a presumption –

MARY. Nevertheless. A faintly ridiculous old soak – isn't that about the size of it – clinging on to the last vestiges of his authority –

CRAIG. That's not what I see at all –

MARY. He has integrity – let me just say that. He insists on telling the truth – and God knows, there have been times – quite recently, actually – when I wished he hadn't. But regardless of his faults and weaknesses – he cares. Deeply.

CRAIG. Mary, I don't want to get off on the wrong foot – with you least of all –

MARY. I agree with you about Taylor Southbury's funeral – I see it for what it is – a very serious problem. But I must ask you to *try* to understand his point of view –

CRAIG. Sure –

MARY. Before you persuade him to abandon his principles, at least allow him that dignity.

CRAIG. Do you think I can persuade him? Honestly?

MARY. We'd better hope you can. Our doctor's wife has just involved herself –

CRAIG. And she's – ?

MARY. An escalation. Take my word for it, there's nothing Janet Oram gets involved in unless it has some guarantee of success... And so far, we've managed to keep things pretty low-key. But if people start drawing attention to the problem – *before* we've had a chance to solve it through careful and sensitive talks...

CRAIG. Mary...

CRAIG *looks back at the back door...*

I'm starting to get a bad feeling about something...

MARY. What?

CRAIG. I think I may have misjudged a situation. I'm sorry.

MARY. What? What situation? What are you talking about?

SUSANNAH *appears again.*

SUSANNAH. I'm going. (*To* CRAIG.) When I get back tonight I can go over the Sunday school stuff.

CRAIG. Oh, that's –

SUSANNAH. I mean if you want to. It's up to you.

CRAIG. Yes. Sure. Whatever. Delighted.

SUSANNAH *starts to go out through the kitchen door.*

MARY. Are you home for dinner?

SUSANNAH (*as she goes*). Where else would I be?

MARY (*to* CRAIG). I'm sorry, You'll have to start from the beginning. I don't understand a word you're saying –

SUSANNAH *comes straight back in – very shocked and shaken.*

SUSANNAH. Jesus Christ.

MARY. Susannah.

SUSANNAH. Get Dad.

MARY. What?

SUSANNAH. Get him.

MARY. What on earth is the matter?

CRAIG. I think perhaps you've spotted the – Yes…

MARY. What is it?

CRAIG. I'm sorry. I thought you knew –

MARY. Knew what?

CRAIG. I thought it was a conscious decision – to leave it there. That's – I'm sorry – that's what I meant earlier – I'm really sorry –

MARY *goes out of the door. We see her look at the house and put her hand over her mouth in horror.*

MARY. Oh my God.

SUSANNAH (*shouting*). Dad!

MARY. Who – in the name of – ?

SUSANNAH (*shouting*). Dad, come down here now!

CRAIG. I'm sorry – I did think it was a little – I wasn't sure…

MARY. You thought it was a 'conscious decision'?

CRAIG. I'm really sorry –

DAVID *appears*.

DAVID. What is it?

SUSANNAH. You need to see this.

DAVID. What?

SUSANNAH. This.

SUSANNAH *goes to the curtains and flings them open. We now see that someone has painted graffiti across the house. We can see part of it – 'U-C-K. Y-O-U'.*

MARY. How long has this been here?

CRAIG. Like I say –

DAVID. You saw it?

CRAIG. Yes –

DAVID. And you didn't think to say anything.

MARY. He thought we knew –

DAVID. Knew?

MARY. Get me some bleach, David. Now.

SUSANNAH *goes to get it.*

CRAIG. I thought you'd seen it and were somehow – I don't know – The archdeacon said something about your pride, about your refusal to be cowed – I see now that was a terrible error on my part –

NAOMI *appears in a T-shirt. She hoots with laughter.*

NAOMI (*laughing*). Oh my God!

MARY (*to DAVID, angrily*). And this is what you call overstated, is it? A storm in a teacup?

NAOMI. The writing's on the wall, Dad.

SUSANNAH. Here, I'll help you.

SUSANNAH *goes to help* MARY, *who is taking the bucket and bleach out to start cleaning.* DAVID *stands, staring.*

NAOMI (*laughing*). The hand of God – What was his name? That king. At the feast. Oh come on, Christians –

DAVID. Belshazzar.

NAOMI. That's him. It never leaves you.

DAVID. 'God has numbered the days of your reign and brought it to an end.'

CRAIG. I'm sorry. Truly. I really should have spoken up.

DAVID. Just go and find a bucket, will you? Welcome to the parish.

CRAIG *rushes to help.* DAVID *stares at the graffiti.*

Black.

3.

Kitchen. Bright, late morning. SUSANNAH *is laying out children's paintings, painted on sugar paper, primary-school style.* JOY SAMPSON, *the local police sergeant, is standing just inside the kitchen in her motorcycle leathers. She's pregnant. She's reading from a sheet of paper.*

JOY (*reading*).
'The vicar is a drunkard
The vicar screws around
The vicar drives his vehicle drunk, all around the town
The vicar is a rascal, but the vicar's gone too far
When Taylor Southbury's laid to rest
The vicar won't be far behind.'

Obviously, he's let himself down with that ending...

SUSANNAH. Who is it, Joy?

JOY. It's anonymous. But with a bit of detective work, I've managed to track down the perpetrator.

SUSANNAH. Who?

JOY. Frank Gillard.

SUSANNAH. Frank Gillard? But he's – We buy our vegetables from him. I teach his granddaughters –

JOY. He obviously nurses a darker side, Susannah.

SUSANNAH. How did you find out?

JOY. He went to a lot of trouble, cutting it all out of a newspaper – But then he stuck it on to his own letter-headed paper.

She holds up the sheet.

SUSANNAH. For God's sake –

JOY. Is that a new skirt?

SUSANNAH. What do you mean?

JOY. I'm just asking. Don't normally see you in a colour, do we?

SUSANNAH. Don't we?

JOY. My Clint calls you 'Sister Susannah'. Not in a mean way –

SUSANNAH. What does that mean – ?

JOY. It means you look like a nun.

SUSANNAH *returns to her pictures, crushed.*

It's not a bad thing. I say to him 'That's the mark of a dedicated teacher, that is. She doesn't care about herself. She's dedicated her every waking minute to them kids.' It's like a – Whatsit?

SUSANNAH (*flatly*). Vocation.

JOY. They've done all these, have they? Your primary class?

SUSANNAH. I thought if I put them out around the meeting there might be some recognition that we aren't all, in fact, heartless brutes.

JOY. You should see their shrine now. Can't move on Raleigh Close for candles and flowers.

SUSANNAH. What do you think will happen, Joy?

JOY. I have no idea. I'll say this, though – I've never seen
anything blow up so fast. Eight days is all – That petition has
ballooned –

SUSANNAH. I hear them up at the school gates – spreading
their nonsense, egging each other on.

JOY. It's just balloons, though, Susannah. Couple of balloons
for a little girl's funeral.

SUSANNAH. It's not a couple.

JOY. I don't understand it. I mean – Yes, it's my job to stay
neutral – but when they're all asking me – 'Is this a hate
crime, Joy? Has he broken some kind of law?'… Oh my
God, I just realised what I said.

SUSANNAH. What?

JOY. Ballooned. 'This petition has ballooned.'

SUSANNAH. Yes – I get it. Thank you, Joy.

JOY. I'll tell you who's really come into his own these past few
days – Your curate. He's a breath of fresh air – That's what
people are saying.

SUSANNAH. He's new, that's all. He hasn't been worn down yet.
(*Looks up at the window.*) Oh God – What am I going to do?

JOY. What do you mean?

SUSANNAH. I can't spend another winter in this place.
I should have left when I had the chance – I should have
travelled.

JOY. We can't lose you, Susannah. We've got no decent
teachers up there as it is.

SUSANNAH. I honestly don't care what they do for my
funeral. They can dissect me in the biology lab, if they like.
Might as well use me as a teaching aid.

JOY. I have to tell you, Susannah. I'm concerned about the river
blessing.

SUSANNAH. Why?

JOY. We have to focus on the safety aspect. He's getting death threats. There's huge crowds of people, emotions running high –

SUSANNAH. Surely it'll all be over by then.

JOY. I'm afraid not – This afternoon he needs to make an apology. He needs to listen. Whose idea was it. Anyway?

SUSANNAH. What?

JOY. This meeting.

SUSANNAH. My mother's. She's off getting crockery now.

JOY. Well, he needs to take it seriously. There's a lot of people coming up here – and they're angry. They expect to be listened to – (*Stops.*) Morning, Mary.

MARY *has come in from the house.*

SUSANNAH. We've had another note.

MARY. What?

SUSANNAH. Frank Gillard.

JOY. And more excrement, I'm afraid.

MARY. No!

JOY. Popped in through the vestry letterbox. Jiffy bag this time. I don't know whether they squat down, or scoop up –

MARY. Alright, Joy. Thank you.

JOY. I don't pretend to understand it, Mary, but I do feel we could use some direction.

MARY. They're all coming here this afternoon. That's the thing that's been missing from all this nonsense – Face-to-face discussion.

MARY *goes and stands at the window, zoning out of the conversation.*

JOY. Is Janet Oram coming?

SUSANNAH. So she says.

JOY. She's made herself very available to the Southburys.
Every morning I see her – driving up to the estate.

SUSANNAH. I'm surprised she knows where it is.

JOY. Whipped them all up on Mumsnet – Started a WhatsApp
group… What's in it for her, that's what I don't understand.

MARY. Your father's with the archdeacon now. He'll come
back with a message of support from the bishop, then
everyone will stop their screaming and shouting, and we can
all get back to normal. Now, what about the chairs?

JOY. For what it's worth, Mary – I've done quite a lot of
reading when it comes to the law –

MARY. I'm glad to hear it.

JOY. And I can't help feeling – this could turn into what's called
a 'non-crime hate incident'.

MARY. A what – ?

JOY. New directives. We're 'a listening force' now, Mary. We
listen to offence – and we take note of it. It's all about 'lived
experience'. You mark my words – the sands are shifting.

MARY. How are you, Joy? How are you feeling?

JOY. I'm alright. (*Pats stomach.*) I'm working up until the last
minute – I don't want to sit on my arse getting anxious all day.

MARY. I'm going to need a bucket.

SUSANNAH. What for?

MARY. I'm presuming the Jiffy bag has left a mess.

JOY. I hate to pour pain upon pain, Mary – but I am going to
have to talk to him about this accident.

MARY. How often is there an accident on Jawbones Hill?

JOY. Very often.

MARY. It's a blind spot.

JOY. I agree. But in this case – he was literally a point under.

MARY. Well, that's still under, isn't it?

JOY. Yes, but I have to speak to him about road safety. It's either that or a course. And the nearest one to us is Newton Abbot, and the bloke who teaches it is a Holocaust denier.

MARY. He'll be back from the archdeacon any minute, Joy –

JOY. I'm coming for the meeting. I'll speak to him then. Good luck with the human waste, Mary. I'll see you later.

She goes. MARY *turns to* SUSANNAH.

MARY. I'm doing a hospice run after the meeting. I'm going to need you to put something in the oven. (*Looks at her.*) Is that a new skirt?

SUSANNAH. I'm trying to brighten myself up.

MARY. And you thought the death of a parishioner's child seemed like the opportune moment.

CRAIG *enters with a parcel.*

CRAIG. Sorry. That all took so much longer than expected.

SUSANNAH. Where have you been?

CRAIG. Fetching parish magazines. Are we – ? (*Looks at watch.*) Yes – Soon – ?

SUSANNAH. Soon-ish.

MARY. I'm going to clean up some mess and then we need to start bringing chairs through.

CRAIG. Is David here?

MARY. He's on his way from the archdeacon. Let's try and get things organised before Janet and her cronies descend. I don't want to be judged any more than I have to be.

She leaves.

CRAIG. I just met her.

SUSANNAH. Janet?

CRAIG. She was leaving the printers. Apparently they're getting some T-shirts made. She seemed very friendly.

SUSANNAH. Oh, she would be. To you. Did she say anything about the funeral?

CRAIG. They're pretty riled up. Your mother seems very –

SUSANNAH. She wants me to change my skirt.

CRAIG. Why?

SUSANNAH. Do you think I look like a nun?

CRAIG. What? No. Anyway, that's one of the things I like about this place. Nobody cares what they look like.

SUSANNAH starts to put up pictures. Hurt.

SUSANNAH. Glowing reviews for your appearance at Year 1 assembly.

CRAIG. Were there?

SUSANNAH. Breathless, even. 'Blessings and gratitude.' I had several of them coming up to me in the course of the day – telling me what their blessings were – why they're grateful…

CRAIG. That's wonderful.

SUSANNAH. I have a question though. From the back of the class.

She raises her hand. CRAIG smiles, signals her to speak.

What about those who… try as they might – *yearn* as they might… just can't feel gratitude. In spite of their spiritual inclination, in spite of… (*Beat.*) What happens to them? The ones who – searching the bottom of their hearts – can only feel a deep-down boiling rage.

She turns away from him to cover the emotion. Beat.

CRAIG. Are you alright?

SUSANNAH. Please. Just answer my question.

CRAIG. What are they feeling rage about? That's what I'd ask. Can they be helped? Can they be reached? Does it have something to do with… what we're talking about…? With blessings?

Beat.

SUSANNAH. It has something to do with the lack of them.

DAVID appears. He has a plastic bag with him.

DAVID. Where's your mother?

SUSANNAH. She's in the church.

CRAIG. Was it alright?

DAVID. What?

CRAIG. The archdeacon? The meeting?

DAVID. Do you mind if I don't talk about it just at the moment?

He sits at the table. MARY comes in.

MARY. What's happened?

DAVID. Where have you been?

MARY. I'm getting chairs from the vestry. What did the archdeacon say?

DAVID. I'm sitting down, Mary. I'm gathering my thoughts.

MARY. Nobody – from this point on – is to come into this room unless they are carrying a chair.

CRAIG. Any chair?

SUSANNAH. I'll show you.

MARY. We need as many as we can – and now, please. This is not a drill. We have very little time.

CRAIG and SUSANNAH leave. Beat. DAVID unpacks his bag – Scotch, fags…

Well – ?

DAVID. I was verbally abused.

MARY. What?

DAVID. Just now. In the Londis. The girl whispered an expletive under her breath.

MARY. You're being paranoid. It probably just sounded like an expletive.

DAVID. I'm sure you're right. What sounds like 'cocksucker'?

MARY. What happened with the archdeacon? Tell me.

DAVID. They said I was tired. That, of course, is a notorious euphemism for 'finished'. The archdeacon fears that I have made a fatal misstep with the parish. She wonders how I will come back from it. She respects my position – naturally – whilst at the same time – as a colleague in Christ – questioning the wisdom of such an intractable stand.

MARY. Did she say that? 'Intractable'?

DAVID. She's a bit more 'Bible in plain English'. She might have said 'solid'.

MARY. Was she angry?

DAVID. We are never angry in the Church of England, Mary. We are grieved.

MARY. Was she grieved?

DAVID. Sorely.

MARY. Did you tell them about the meeting? About this afternoon?

DAVID. I did.

MARY. And what did they say?

DAVID. They were pleased. They rejoiced. Is this a pie?

MARY. I thought it better to offer some kind of refreshment, even if they don't eat it.

Silence.

DAVID. I believe you received a letter.

MARY. Who told you about that?

DAVID. Your correspondent sent a copy to the diocese. It was sitting on the table when I arrived.

MARY. Would you like to see it?

DAVID *shakes his head.* MARY *produces a crumpled letter from her pocket and puts it in front of him.*

DAVID. It's not true. The day I told you... The day I promised I would never meet with her again... was the last time I ever saw her alone –

MARY. I know.

DAVID. This is a spiteful lie.

Beat.

MARY. I want you to apologise this afternoon –

DAVID. Mary –

MARY. I want you to give her her wretched balloons. I don't know what sleight of hand you practised with the archdeacon – But – I can see this, David. I'm three steps ahead of you. And I can see it unravelling right in front of our eyes.

DAVID (*quietly*). I can't...

MARY. What?

DAVID. Go against my own conscience.

MARY. Why not? What's so special about *your* conscience? And why now particularly? Let's face it, it's hardly been the most steadfast of guides.

She takes back the letter as evidence of this.

DAVID. Mary –

MARY. This is my home. It may be imperfect – God knows – but it's mine. And I refuse to be turfed out – I *refuse* to be evicted – over the *one single principle* you happen to think worth fighting for.

CRAIG *comes in. He has two plastic chairs with him.*

CRAIG. These chairs are good. Nice and light in case someone decides to throw one.

Silence. DAVID and MARY lost in their own worlds.

Sorry. That was a joke.

MARY. Are you changing your clothes?

DAVID. Yes.

MARY. Then change.

She goes. CRAIG *looks at* DAVID. *A little silence then –*

DAVID. When I first came to this living the outgoing priest gave me two pieces of advice. The first was about parking. The second was an exhortation on the first principles of ecclesiastical responsibility...

CRAIG. Which are?

DAVID. 'Don't fuck the flock'... (*Beat.*) Come to think of it, his advice about parking was pretty spot-on, too.

A little silence. DAVID *looks at him.*

Mary thinks I should apologise – No – Mary demands that I apologise.

CRAIG. She's right.

DAVID. She's wrong. She knows she's wrong. But that's not the point.

CRAIG. I don't understand you, David. What are you holding out for – ? The days of – whatever – the paternal parish priest –

DAVID. It isn't that –

CRAIG. Explain it to me, then.

DAVID. Integrity. Is that an explanation? The integrity of the church.

CRAIG. It is. And it's very laudable. But are you absolutely sure?

DAVID. Sure?

CRAIG. Sometimes our motivations disguise themselves. Sometimes – what we perceive as integrity – is actually a kind of vanity.

Silence. DAVID *regards him.*

DAVID. Tomorrow evening, we'll be blessing the river. Wait till you see – It's the biggest house I play to. Locals, visitors, grockles... Bigger than Christmas. Why? *Why* do they all come? It's a ceremony that's as old as the settlement here –

almost certainly pre-Christian. We putter out to the mouth –
to the point where the river meets the sea... That's – For the
fishing fleet, I mean – for the trawlers – That's the deadliest
stretch. If you go overboard, there, the undertow will take
you. The bodies are never found. 'The river claims a life a
year.' That's what they say... And I bless the dark, raging
water. (*Beat.*) Why am I telling you this? That ceremony – a
ceremony, which – as you can probably tell – I happen to
rather like – is compelling to people because it brings them
closer to the truth. The *truth*, Craig. Death is death. It's not
balloons, it's not Disneyland...

CRAIG. Of course, I agree with you. In principle – But in this
particular case –

DAVID. Why not cave in? Why not just let them have their
balloons? Because I'd be giving them what they wanted. Not
what they need. And that would be a dereliction of my duty.

CRAIG. That's quite a presumption. To know what they need
better than they do.

DAVID. Everybody thinks – in situations like this – tragic,
terrible circumstances – that what they need is a hug. And
they do – Oh God, they do. But not *just* a hug. And not from
me. I have to give them more than that – I have to...
something that will last after the flowers and the cards – and
all the attention, and the poems – after all of that – has
passed away... This is more important than the usual
wrangles – Believe me... The inappropriate headstone, the
ridiculous baptismal names –

CRAIG. In other circumstances, I might agree with you. I'm
sorry. But in your particular case –

DAVID. You mean –

CRAIG. I can't find a better way to say it. You're not exactly
the poster boy for unshakeable principles, David. I'm sorry.
You're not.

DAVID. No.

A little silence. CRAIG *makes to go.* DAVID *is suddenly
fierce. Cruel, even.*

Satisfy my curiosity, will you? Has anything ever ruffled that benign exterior? I'm struggling to picture it, you see?

CRAIG. I'm sorry to hear that.

DAVID. So will your parishioners be. Because – my principles may be shaky – but when a man comes to me and says 'I pulled up onto the hard shoulder, Father, and chugged a bottle of Scotch at eight a.m.' – I can look him square in the eye and say, 'Me too, brother. Me fucking too.'

Beat, as he instantly regrets it.

I'm sorry –

CRAIG. No –

DAVID. That was unforgivable.

CRAIG *goes to the door –*

I'm sorry. I'm so sorry.

CRAIG *turns, conciliatory –*

CRAIG. My first post was in Highbury. Just near the Arsenal stadium. We had an endless battle over headstones. I wanted to hand out leaflets with the death certificate – 'Things you may have on your gravestone: A cross. Things you may not have: Arsene Wenger.'

DAVID. I'm sorry, Craig. I should never – That was wrong of me.

CRAIG. I've chugged from a bottle at eight a.m., David. In my case it was usually wine. I've swallowed mouthwash to cover it up at meetings, I've hidden stashes... My parents... I think the first time I picked up a drink I was eight years old...

DAVID. This is none of my business –

CRAIG. Who knows? If you ever want to... (*Beat.*) I'm here, David. If you ever want to know how I stopped – You only have to ask. I hope one day you will. I pray for it, in fact.

DAVID *nods.*

DAVID. I had to refuse a baptismal name a few years ago. They cancelled the christening.

CRAIG. What name did they want?

DAVID. Pagan.

> CRAIG *smiles. He goes.* DAVID *alone for a second.*

> *(Half-whispering, flatly, intoning).* Lord Jesus Christ... Son of God... Have mercy on me, a sinner...

> *He takes a large glass of Scotch – already filled and hidden – from the cupboard and drains it.*

> Lord Jesus Christ... Son of God...

> LEE *appears at the back door.* DAVID *hides the drink.*

LEE. Alright, Vicar.

DAVID. Lee – Come in. Do you want something – ? Food or something? There's a pie –

LEE. I just had a full English at The Old Jerusalem. Bob Sykes cooked it for me. He's a twat, actually – but he's drummed up a lot of support for us. He's got one of the stickers in his window. 'Justice for Taylor.'

DAVID. It's not about justice –

LEE. Most people think it is. There's talk of news crews, Vicar. National interest –

DAVID. Have you spoken to your mum? What did she say?

LEE. She's posted something on my Facebook.

DAVID. Yes?

LEE. She wishes I'd died and Taylor'd lived. She says I'm a sick fuck. She got six hundred and eighty likes.

> JANET *knocks and appears at the door.* LEE *scurries to the corner.*

JANET. Oh, David –

DAVID. Good afternoon, Janet.

JANET. Do you know the overwhelming feeling I had, walking over here?

DAVID. Please. Tell me.

JANET. Immense sadness.

DAVID. Well, at least on that, we can both agree.

They shake hands.

JANET. What's it all about? Honestly. Is it pride? Nostalgia?

DAVID. It's about my responsibility as a priest.

JANET. You don't think your responsibility extends to a young woman going through the most appalling loss imaginable.

DAVID. I think that sounds like rather a loaded question.

JANET. I get it, David. Balloons. They're… It's not exactly my taste either. And the girl –

DAVID. It has nothing to do with taste –

JANET. Tina is not an easy person. I know that too. I've spent most of this week with her. And, my Peter… this is strictly between ourselves… had the most dreadful time when she first brought Taylor into the surgery –

LEE. Did she say anything about me?

JANET *starts.*

JANET. Jesus, Lee. I didn't – What are you doing there, skulking in corners?

LEE. Did she say anything about me?

JANET. No. She didn't mention you once. And frankly, I don't blame her.

LEE. You could put in a good word for me, though? Couldn't you, Mrs Oram? You could tell her I'm sorry?

DAVID. I think it would be terrifically helpful if you could.

JANET. It's out of the question.

LEE. Why?

JANET. Because – Why don't you think about your behaviour, Lee? How about that for a 'why'? Think about the terrible hurt you've caused –

DAVID. Is Tina on her way?

JANET. I don't know. I don't know if she'll come at all.

DAVID. What do you mean?

JANET. She's angry, David. And she's not the only one. God knows, if this was one of my children – (*Beat*.) Why won't you just give in? Give in – and admit what this is really about.

DAVID. What is it really about?

JANET. Power.

DAVID. Power?

JANET. You've made your point, haven't you? – You've lodged your objection – Why persist? Why make yourself into the town ogre?

DAVID. I agree with you. I do. I have done everything wrong – Everything. And I'm sorry –

JANET. Good –

DAVID. I'm sorry. Truly. For every piece of hurt I've caused –

MARY *enters,* SUSANNAH *and* CRAIG *behind*.

MARY. What's going on? Where's Tina?

DAVID. Apparently there's no guarantee she's going to appear.

MARY (*to* JANET). What – ? But that's ridiculous.

CRAIG. Lee, surely you can speak to her.

JANET. He's the last person she's going to listen to.

JOY *appears*.

JOY. Right. Are we starting? Because I've got Brownies at quarter-to.

DAVID. Janet was just asking me to admit what this is really about, Mary.

MARY. What on earth does that mean?

JANET. Not now, David. That's – We were alone –

DAVID. No – please – Isn't this supposed to be an open debate? Power. That's what you said –

MARY. Power?

JANET. Alright... It's a punishment. Isn't it? 'The dog in the manger.' You're struggling away in an empty church, and... Look, we had some friends, recently, who got married in a crop circle –

LEE. What are they, scarecrows?

JANET (*tersely*). They're biodynamic farmers. She writes a wine column... The point is... People aren't afraid to define their landmark moments any more. To individualise... And that's – It's humiliating for you. I get it. So when someone actually wants to *use* the church – use it and *fill* it for once – you lay down a whole load of restrictions. I'm not saying I don't understand it –

MARY. I think you very clearly don't understand it.

JANET. And it's not just this, David. It's all the other stuff –

She fishes in her bag to produce a list –

DAVID. Other stuff?

JANET. The Nativity – Banning mobile phones...

DAVID. Is this a list?

JANET. I told you. People are angry... (*List again.*) The music you choose, the morbid business with the cross every Easter –

MARY. The stations of the cross are, rather necessarily, morbid –

JANET. But is there not a case – Hear me out – for accepting the fact that most people – rightly or wrongly – see the church as a building – a backdrop? I know that sounds harsh, but – it's true. Isn't it? How many people that you marry, or christen, or bury, are really – genuinely – thinking about Christianity?

DAVID. It's rather difficult to gauge with the people I bury –

JANET. There you go again. (*The list.*) High-handed.
    Patronising...

DAVID. I'm sorry –

CRAIG. He is listening. Aren't you, David?

JANET. I think you actually do a lot of good. I really do. I'm
    not religious, myself, but – I suppose I would describe
    myself as 'spiritual'... And I think a lot of the general stuff
    around Christianity is positive, on the whole –

DAVID. Thank you.

JANET. But, really – in the light of all that – What could it
    possibly matter to you – tell me, honestly – if that poor girl
    gets her balloons?

DAVID. Janet, I hear your assessment of my character – the
    town's assessment – and I agree. And worse. I am a failure –

MARY. David –

DAVID. I have committed every possible sin – Pride – Yes.
    Arrogance – Absolutely. I am guilty, and I am ashamed of it.
    I drink. Often. I have broken my vows – to God, to my
    family... To my wife –

MARY. David, please –

DAVID. I have been an idiot – an arsehole. A cheat. But I'm
    begging you, Janet. Please. Please. *Try* to understand what
    I'm saying –

MARY. David, pull yourself together.

JANET. I think he's actually drunk.

LEE (*amused*). Good for you, Vicar! Let's all have one! Liven
    things up a bit!

DAVID. The point is – I want you to try and understand. If *this*
    doesn't matter – This principle – this thing that I'm trying to
    express... then nothing does.

JANET. What – ?

DAVID. Nothing.

JANET. You're not making any sense.

DAVID. Then listen. If this doesn't matter –

MARY. David, stop it.

DAVID. Then nothing does.

CRAIG. I think we should all just take a moment. Sit down. Gather ourselves.

DAVID. What do you want me to do? Apologise? I apologise. Unreservedly. Do you want me to kneel?

He does. NAOMI *has entered –*

MARY. David, get up.

DAVID. I'll kneel. But please –

NAOMI. What the fuck is he doing – ?

MARY. David, I thought we'd agreed –

DAVID. My wife wants me to give in – to allow these balloons –

MARY (*furious*). David!

DAVID (*to* MARY). No, it's good. It's good that they know. (*To* JANET.) But… For reasons that are bigger than both of us – reasons I am scarcely able to articulate – please, *please* believe me when I say – this is not just a question of taste – of mere aesthetics. It's about insisting on the best. No – not the best – the authentic. The real. The true. A fullness of life – which – if you'll forgive me for bringing him up – is what Jesus was banging on about. Elitist though it may be, arrogant though it doubtless appears – I am pleading for nothing less than an experience which is worthy of God. *God.* And if that doesn't matter – If that can be swept aside like a detail – then nothing matters. Nothing. And if anyone has something to say which carries more weight than that – I'd be happy to hear them.

TINA (*offstage*). Do you ever remember meeting her?

They all turn to reveal TINA SOUTHBURY. *She's at the door, holding a pink child's scooter. She looks drawn, ill.*

DAVID. Tina –

He gets up.

TINA. I was wondering if you remembered –

DAVID. I –

TINA. You met her at a ballet thing at the primary. You gave her a cup. She hadn't won it, they all got one. It was only for a minute, but – I wondered if you remembered.

DAVID. Of course... I'm sorry. I didn't –

TINA. It was like, five seconds. Why would you?

SUSANNAH. Hello, Tina.

JOY. You alright, Tina?

JANET. Tina, where have you been? Are you okay?

TINA. I took this off the fence. Someone wired it on there with all the flowers and the kids' toys and that. 'A present for Taylor.' Well, it's no use to her now, is it? My other kids would kill for one of these... It's brand new... There's nothing wrong with me taking it for my other kids, is there? Do you know what these things cost? It's not like Taylor can fucking ride it, is it? Why shouldn't I take it?

SUSANNAH. How are you feeling, Tina?

TINA. Some bloke called Choudry's donated a load more balloons. Indian. He runs a party shop in Exeter. Saw it in the paper – I never asked him to... You can have anything you want in their religion. You can have fairy lights and all sorts in their church. You can have balloons or anything you want.

DAVID. I'm very glad you're here, Tina. I hope that now we can have a proper talk.

TINA. Hello, Mary.

MARY. Hello, Tina.

TINA. You sent some meals up. That was kind.

MARY. I've got some more here. I've frozen them. Just something for the children. You can take them when you go.

LEE. You should hear some of the stuff he's been coming out with, Tina. It's unbelievable.

TINA. How's Clint, Joy?

JOY. He's not too bad, thanks.

TINA. I saw him Wednesday. Got balder, hasn't he?

JOY. Not a hair on his head. I know some women find that sexy, but –

TINA. Not you?

JOY. It's like making love to a muscular baby.

DAVID. Tina, why don't you take a seat?

TINA. You're Naomi. Naomi Highland.

NAOMI. Yes. Hello… I'm… I'm sorry about your little girl…

TINA. We saw you in that thing about demons. What was it called? Me and my mum watched it. You bit that bloke's neck after you'd shagged him.

NAOMI. I… Yeah.

TINA. Can I have a selfie?

NAOMI. Sorry – ?

TINA. Will you do a selfie or what? Yes or no?

NAOMI. Oh. I – Yes. Sure.

LEE. I'll take it if you want, Tina. Me and Naomi was mates at school.

NAOMI. No, we weren't. Mates?

LEE. Yeah –

NAOMI. What are you – delusional?

LEE. Until you went off to boarding school and turned into a right little madam.

NAOMI. We were mates until you started some pretty choice name-calling – as I recall. I hope you don't need me to repeat them.

DAVID. What – ?

MARY. Is this true – ?

LEE. She's lying, Vicar. She's totally lying.

DAVID. Lee, why is it that every time I learn something new about you it turns out to be appalling?

TINA holds the phone out and takes the picture – without smiling. NAOMI smiles, uncomfortably.

TINA. You like it, do you? Acting?

NAOMI. I'm not sure. I'm actually thinking of giving up.

TINA. Well, don't do it till I've posted this. I want people to know who the fuck you are.

NAOMI nods. Okay. Silence. TINA puts away her phone and looks round the room.

I want everyone to go except the vicar... Everyone.

CRAIG. Tina, I'm really a neutral eye on this whole thing –

TINA. I don't care what you are – you can fuck off too. All of you.

JANET. Tina –

TINA. Everyone.

JANET (*hugging her*). I'll be up in the morning, I'll see you then. And do persist with the magnesium. It really does help with grief.

They leave. MARY stays, LEE too.

MARY. I'm not going, Tina.

LEE. Neither am I –

TINA (*to LEE*). I don't give a fuck what you do... (*To DAVID.*) I've been going through loads of old photos. Trying to find a picture of Taylor for the cover of the... thing – the service – whatever it's called.

DAVID. I expect that was very tough.

LEE. I would have done it if you'd asked me. I've got loads of pictures. I've got some really nice ones on my phone.

MARY. Tina, David has something he wants to say to you.

TINA. Oh, yeah?

DAVID. I want to apologise. I want to express how sorry I am –

TINA. You gonna let me have my balloons, then?

Silence.

DAVID. No. I'm sorry.

MARY (*quietly*). David –

DAVID. I don't think they'll help you, Tina. I'm sorry.

TINA. I want them.

DAVID. I've buried lots and lots of people, Tina. Old and young. I believe that this is what's best – not just for the service, for the present – but for the future... If it's the church you want... My church –

TINA. It is.

DAVID. Then there are reasons for things... Traditions...

MARY. David, for God's sake –

TINA. Listen, I want the church, because she deserves the church.

DAVID. I agree.

TINA. She needs a send-off. She was... She was a proper character, Vicar... She loved the drama, I'm telling you. She loved all... She loved... She was a show-off. Actually. A proper madam. Even at the hospital they were all...

LEE. She could have been on TV.

TINA. She deserves the church.

DAVID. Then let me give her the funeral that is worthy of her. And let me prepare a place where you can mourn. (*Beat.*) We can't hide from it, Tina – That's what I'm saying. We can't dress it up. Because the truth – however terrible – has to be faced. This dreadful ceremony belongs to grief. And it's better we face that together, at the *moment* of committal. Grief. And love. *That's* what the ritual is for.

TINA. That won't mean anything to her.

DAVID. I think it will.

TINA. It won't mean anything to me…

Starts to leave.

DAVID. Please. Don't go.

TINA. Can I have my balloons?

DAVID. No. I'm sorry.

TINA. Then I've nothing left to say.

LEE. I need to speak to Mum.

TINA. You'll give her a wide berth if you know what's good for you.

LEE. I don't know why I said it, Tina. I don't.

MARY. Don't go, Tina. Stay.

TINA makes to leave.

LEE. But do you forgive me? Do you forgive me, Tina? Have *you* forgiven me?… Tina?

TINA (*to* DAVID). You've let me down, Vicar.

DAVID. I believe that I've done the opposite.

TINA. You were so kind in the hospital. I couldn't believe how nice you were. I thought – this is what they mean – all this fucking shit about Jesus – this is what they're on about.

LEE. Tina –

TINA. I can't believe you'd be so cruel after you've been so nice.

DAVID. I have to follow my conscience.

TINA. Fuck you, and fuck your conscience.

She spits on the floor.

LEE. Tina – ?

TINA. I hope one day you'll feel this – what I feel.

LEE (*distraught*). Tina, I've got nowhere to go tonight, nowhere to stay.

TINA. I hope it happens soon, and I hope it drags your guts out like this.

DAVID. Tina, please –

She spits at DAVID.

TINA. Cunt.

She leaves.

LEE. Tina –

He follows her out. MARY *goes to the sink and gets a tea towel. She gently wipes* DAVID*'s face. After a moment, she comes to a stop. They stare at each other.*

DAVID. Mary –

MARY. No. Not this time.

She walks away, dropping the tea towel by the sink.

You won't stop me leaving this time.

She leaves. DAVID *stands alone.*

End of Act One.

ACT TWO

4.

NAOMI *and* CRAIG. *Late afternoon.* CRAIG *is in full priest garb.* NAOMI *is dressed to go out. Outside we might be able to hear the hubbub from the blessing of the river crowd. Maybe the boom of music from the pub. The odd flare going off...*

NAOMI. 'Anglicanism.' 'Anglican.' Funny word, isn't it? I mean... it's literally... the religion of being English... 'Thou shalt not express thy feelings. Thou shalt bury them with gin and stinging irony'... Would you like to hear an Anglican joke?

CRAIG. I didn't know – ?

NAOMI. How many Anglicans does it take to change a light bulb?

CRAIG. Tell me.

NAOMI. Three. One to change the bulb, one to mix the drinks, and one to say the old bulb was better and why can't they leave things the way they *were*. Does it bother you that I'm drinking?

CRAIG. Does it bother you that I'm not?

NAOMI. Oh, very good. Very psychological... Top of the vicaring class for that one... I can stop if you like – I don't want to tempt you... Like Salomé.

CRAIG. I'm tempted every day. I just don't have one. And you stopping wouldn't make the slightest bit of difference.

NAOMI. Because you've beaten your body into submission?

CRAIG. I'm sorry?

NAOMI. What else is going on? The tennis, the five a.m. runs.

CRIAG. I – I'm sorry. I didn't realise – Do I wake you?

NAOMI. Wake me? I'm just getting in, love... Tiptoeing past my dad on his little camp bed...

CRAIG. That must be strange.

NAOMI *shrugs*.

NAOMI. They've slept in separate rooms before... I'll tell you something, though – This time's different.

CRAIG. You think she'll leave.

NAOMI. I know she will. Take my word for it. Le marriage est terminé. Anyway, let's not talk about them. It's depressing.

A little silence.

CRAIG. You were telling me about the agency.

NAOMI. Was I? 'The origin story'? (*Beat.*) Have you ever been to one of those adoption agencies? They really *are* the living embodiment of the good old C of E... Understated. Well meaning. Propped up by women in cardigans who don't take a salary... (*An imitation.*) 'Nowadays, of course, it wouldn't happen like that.' They were very keen to impress upon me what a bleak, colonial throwback I was.

CRAIG. Oh?

NAOMI. 'We would never place a black child with white parents. Our guidelines have been comprehensively updated'... I shouldn't be mean about her, she was perfectly fine. Just embarrassed. Falling over herself to tell me how they've 'decolonised the process'. I should've said 'Listen, love – I don't give a fuck about the process, I just want to' – What? What did I want? That's the problem...

CRAIG. Did you find her?

NAOMI. Eventually. She was a student nurse. Only seventeen. Imagine how terrified she was... No one ever knew how to do my hair here... That's – I wanted to look at her hair, her skin... I wanted to see myself in it... And I did, I suppose.

NAOMI *breaks the mood – another drink, maybe a cigarette...*

(*Suddenly animated.*) God! *Why* have I come home? Is there anything more depressing than waking up in your childhood bedroom?

CRAIG. People dream about that. They sing about it.

NAOMI. Who? John Denver? He didn't have to wake up to a ceiling full of gymkhana rosettes...

CRAIG. So why did you?

NAOMI. What?

CRAIG. Come home.

NAOMI. I wanted to look at myself. Here. I wanted to... See who I was. Am. (*Beat.*) And, besides – Since we're trading confidences –

CRAIG. There hasn't been much trading.

NAOMI. Your time will come. There's a man.

CRAIG. Is there?

NAOMI. With a very fast car. Entirely unsuitable –

CRAIG. In what way?

NAOMI. He's married. There now – I've finally scandalised you.

CRAIG. I grew up in Dalmarnock. It takes a lot more than that to scandalise me.

A flare goes off on the river, illuminating the room with colour for a second.

NAOMI. I used to enjoy the river blessing. I was sitting in London, and I thought – I should go home. See the blessing. That'll be nice. Instead I've spent the day wandering from one dismal pub to another. (*Lifts her glass.*) 'Saudade.'

CRAIG. Saudade?

NAOMI. It's a Portuguese word. It means... Longing. But not. Longing for a place that never existed. They're very romantic, the Portuguese. They're even romantic about sardines. What time is it?

CRAIG. Ten-to.

NAOMI. Nearly showtime… It's awash with longing, this town.
I expect you've noticed. Longing, and boredom. Bored, bored
bored, the poor things. 'Aburrida, aburrida.' That's not
Portuguese. It's Spanish. I drift effortlessly between
languages. It's also possible, I may have become intoxicated.

CRAIG. Well, it is a festival after all.

NAOMI. It is for you.

CRAIG. What do you mean?

NAOMI. Sliding into pole position so effortlessly. Taking my
father's place in his favourite service.

CRAIG. That was the last thing I wanted. Truly.

NAOMI. He thinks the police warnings were exaggerated.

CRAIG. He'll be here in a minute – I think perhaps he'll tell
you how hard he had to persuade me –

NAOMI. Oh, spare me that speech, darling. I've had enough
understudies to know the truth. You were just itching to
wriggle into his tights and skip downstage. I'll tell you
something, though. I don't agree.

CRAIG. You don't –

NAOMI. I don't think they were exaggerated at all… I know
this place, you see. I know it better than anyone in this
family. If anything, the police were underestimating. I think
if he set one foot outside that door, he'd be ripped limb from
limb. (*Beat.*) You're a bit of a puzzle, aren't you?

CRAIG. Am I?

NAOMI. All this. What did you do before?

CRAIG. I was a teacher. Briefly. Not a good one. Not as good
as your sister.

NAOMI. But how did you escape?

CRAIG. Escape?

NAOMI. You're a long way from home, Dorothy.

CRAIG. An English teacher. A wee gay boy from the east end of Glasgow, I hadn't much choice but to escape.

NAOMI. Wait. I was right about you being an understudy...
But I was wrong about the part.

CRAIG. Oh?

NAOMI. It's not my dad you're covering. It's me.

CRAIG. I'm sorry, I don't –

NAOMI. I mean you're a different *type* of outsider – a different *flavour* – Perhaps you haven't noticed yet.

Silence. NAOMI *crosses the room and puts her scarf around his neck. He looks a little alarmed but smiles.*

CRAIG. What's this?

NAOMI. I was once in your shoes. Now I anoint you with my experience. I bless you with it... 'Glory be to God for dappled things. All things counter, original, spare, strange...' And if you're in the business of taking advice –

CRAIG. Of course.

NAOMI. Then, as long as you don't allow yourself to believe the – What shall I call it – delusion – You'll get on just fine.

CRAIG. Delusion?

NAOMI. I mean this kindly. They're not... The people in this town are actually quite decent. Mostly. And they will cherish you, in their own uptight, little way. But... Am I speaking out of turn?

CRAIG. Please –

NAOMI. This is where the delusion comes in – What you are to them is a living, breathing proof of their 'open-mindedness'. The gay vicar. 'Oh we love the gay vicar. We have him over all the time.' 'We prefer him, actually. It's a breath of fresh air.' (*Beat.*) I used to go to people's houses – other children's houses – This isn't a sob story... and I would hear the mothers competing on how little it mattered to them that I was the vicar's little black girl. 'They don't see colour, do they? The little ones. They're such a lesson.'

CRAIG. That sounds very wearing.

NAOMI. Yes. It will be.

Silence. SUSANNAH *comes in, dressed as a verger for the service.*

SUSANNAH. Where's Dad?

CRAIG. The vestry?

SUSANNAH. And where have you been all day?

NAOMI. I've been in town. I've been to the yacht club and The Old Jerusalem. Now I'm going for a drive – with a man whose name escapes me – and we're going to smoke weed and watch the fireworks from a hill.

SUSANNAH. Which hill?

NAOMI. Jawbones? Gallant's Bower? The highest I can find.

SUSANNAH. What the hell is he doing in the vestry?

CRAIG. He's picking out some board games.

SUSANNAH. What?

NAOMI. So he can spend the rest of the evening playing Buckaroo with his racist friend, Lee Southbury.

SUSANNAH. And where's Mum?

NAOMI. I have no idea. Having a little nap in her tomb, I expect.

JANET *appears at the back door.*

JANET. I need to speak to Joy Sampson.

NAOMI. Joy Sampson doesn't live here, Janet.

JANET. I know that. Thank you. There's no one at the station.

SUSANNAH. I expect she'll be on patrol.

CRAIG. Is it urgent?

JANET. My car's been towed.

SUSANNAH *and* NAOMI *both turn away to hide their smirks.*

CRAIG. Oh, goodness. That's very frustrating.

NAOMI. Were you double-parked?

JANET. I was parked outside the surgery. In Peter's designated space. Honestly, the way this town operates with regard to motorists –

CRAIG. It's extremely difficult.

JANET. It's intolerable. As if this silly river business isn't insane enough – visitors crawling all over...

NAOMI. I'm surprised you aren't wearing one of your T-shirts.

JANET (*with mounting strain*). They haven't arrived yet. I told them not to do it on the cheap – And now we're going to end up with something completely unsustainable made by child slaves in Bangladesh –

She turns her head away. Stressed tears appearing. They exchange glances.

CRAIG. Janet, are you okay?

JANET. I'm fine. (*Turns back – a brave face.*) Take my word for it, Craig, there's nothing like winter in a summer town for really messing with your serotonin.

CRAIG. Why don't you come in for a minute. Sit down.

JANET shakes her head.

JANET (*breathes out*). Will you please tell Joy that I'm looking for her.

CRAIG. We absolutely will – If we see her. Of course.

JANET. Thank you, Craig. Thank you.

She goes.

NAOMI. Jesus.

CRAIG. I feel sorry for her.

SUSANNAH. Why?

CRAIG. Can't you see how lonely she is.

NAOMI. Well, that can happen when you're a snooty bitch.

NAOMI *fetches a bottle of gin out of a cupboard.*

SUSANNAH. I suppose you have to take that, do you?

NAOMI. I'm afraid I do. Goodbye, Christians. I hope that big black river doesn't swallow you up.

She goes. SUSANNAH *holds out a life jacket to* CRAIG.

SUSANNAH. You're going to need this.

CRAIG. Am I?

SUSANNAH. We all wear one. In case of emergencies. (*Puts it on.*) You mustn't worry. I'll be there. I've done it a thousand times. It's all about balance – remember? You're going to be fine.

DAVID *comes in, he's carrying a box of board games.* MARY *following.*

DAVID. Aha. Here you are.

SUSANNAH. I'm going to get them ready – Are the choir standing by?

MARY. Not all of them. They may need flushing out of the pub.

SUSANNAH. Oh for heaven's sake –

SUSANNAH *goes.*

MARY. Have you imparted your wisdom?

DAVID. Not yet.

MARY. Keep a neutral tone.

DAVID. Oh, yes that's important.

MARY. No emotion. No Tony Blair.

CRAIG. I'm sorry, I don't –

DAVID. Never read the Bible like you mean it. Politicians do that – it's a trick you must avoid. Just let the words wash over them. It's not about you. And don't try to convince anybody it's about them, either. It's bigger than that. It's impersonal.

CRAIG. Right. Yes. Absolutely.

MARY. I'll go and make sure they're ready.

She leaves. DAVID *looks at him.*

DAVID. You might inspire more confidence if you put the life jacket on *after* you've got into the boat.

CRAIG. I'm not a strong swimmer.

DAVID. Swimming is not a requirement. In fact, if you find yourself swimming, you may safely conclude that you've failed.

CRAIG. Susannah says it's all about balance.

DAVID. And so it is.

CRAIG. I'm still not confident with the service –

DAVID. You walk in procession to the river. The cross is in front of you, the choir behind. Most people behave pretty well, but there'll be the odd jeer as you pass the pub. One or two of them may moon –

CRAIG. Moon?

DAVID. Make the sign of the cross over their exposed buttocks, that tends to shut them up. The majority of the town will follow behind the choir –

CRAIG. Really – ?

DAVID. Oh, it's a very popular event. Once you get to the quay, a gentleman called Jack Tremlett will help you on to a dinghy – Now he may be the worse for drink, but, don't panic, he's a very competent oarsman.

CRAIG. Right –

DAVID. From there you'll be transferred – quite safely – on to a fishing trawler, moored in the middle of the river –

CRAIG. Are you sure you wouldn't be better off doing it yourself – ? A lot of people think the police are exaggerating –

DAVID. Craig. I have the utmost faith in you. You will excel at this. You will do it so well that they will dispense with me altogether. Believe it.

CRAIG. Thank you.

Beat. In the distance the sound of hymn singing.

They're coming.

DAVID. Yes.

CRAIG *gets to the door. Turns.*

CRAIG. Mary said that the order of service is held out in front of me –

DAVID. By the verger, yes. Susannah will do it.

CRAIG. Couldn't I hold it myself?

DAVID. What?

CRAIG. Well, the boat will be moving – It'll be very hard to read. Wouldn't it be easier if I dispensed with the formalities and just held the sheet myself?

DAVID. 'Dispensed with the formalities'? What do you think this is? The fucking Methodists?

CRAIG. Sorry.

DAVID. Go.

CRAIG. Sorry. Yes. Sorry. I'm so sorry.

He does.

DAVID. 'Dispense with the formalities.'

MARY *comes in.*

MARY. Very strange. You not being down there.

DAVID. Well, let's not start getting sentimental.

MARY. 'We ask God to bless our livelihood. Our river. We ask him to protect our sons who work on it. We throw bread into the water so that the fish will leave untouched, the bodies of those we have lost.'

Silence. They look at each other.

DAVID. The house is empty.

MARY *nods*.

When I went to the archdeacon, she asked me something I was unable to answer.

MARY. Oh?

DAVID. She asked if you were happy.

MARY. Well, that was an impertinent enquiry. What did you say?

DAVID. They think it's important, Mary. As a matter of fact, so do I...

MARY. Well, it's none of her business. And I hope you said so.

DAVID. When I think about my behaviour... Especially toward you –

MARY. Don't –

MARY *moves away*.

DAVID. Everything I've done – Everything I've failed to do...

MARY. David –

DAVID. I have such shame, Mary. Such regret. Most of all, I'm ashamed of how unhappy I've made my family.

MARY. The girls aren't unhappy.

DAVID. I was too hard on Susannah. I pushed her. Naomi too.

MARY. At least you were warm. I had no talent for that. For fun. I suppose we do what we were taught...

'Happy.' I remember when happiness was something that came over one as a surprise... Now it's something we're all obligated to be all the time. Like hydrated... I went to the shrine this morning.

DAVID. Weren't you afraid of being set upon?

MARY. They don't notice me. Anyway, it was early.

DAVID. I expect it's grown.

MARY. It has. It's even attracting tourists.

DAVID. Tourists?

MARY. Oh, it's quite the magnet. Stop off on your way to the blessing. Take a selfie… It's funny – the little devotions have totally parted company with reality now. Baby things everywhere – booties, rattles… Little key rings from remote places – I don't know what they're about … Candles, of course –

DAVID. And balloons.

MARY. Oh, hundreds of balloons.

DAVID. I hope it's good for business.

MARY. Whose?

DAVID. Shrines and martyrdoms were always a boon for local merchants. Whole medieval towns sprung up. Perhaps one day we'll be standing on the site of the Church of Taylor Southbury. The Cathedral, even. Perhaps the town will be renamed for her. A World Heritage Site. If so, it rather begs the question – why object to it?

MARY. I wasn't always absolutely faithful. I think you deserve to know that… I think you suspected –

DAVID. Roger Macklin.

MARY. No. Not him. We were friends – I knew you didn't believe me – We were friends.

DAVID. You had a sort of closeness. It made me jealous.

MARY. That was horses. And I suppose he made me laugh. No, I'm talking about my course.

DAVID. What course? The medieval poets?

MARY. Elizabethan. Yes.

DAVID. But that was…

MARY. Oh, I was young –

DAVID. What was his name?

MARY. What could that possibly matter now? He was a fellow student.

DAVID. Susannah could only have been... Your mother was still alive. She was helping while you were away...

MARY. It was pre-Naomi. It wasn't a real affair. Not like yours. It was... I was unfaithful in my heart. I allowed myself to imagine a life away from you. Away from Susannah too. (*Beat.*) My God, I wish...

DAVID. What?

MARY. I wish it had been real.

Beat.

DAVID. Another life.

A little silence.

MARY. What did you do with her? When you – What did you do?

DAVID. Do?

MARY. How did you spend your time?

DAVID. She was... I found her company...

MARY. Tell me.

DAVID. Light. Easy. Easier.

MARY. Yes, I've never been light.

DAVID. She had a habit of saying whatever came into her mind – whatever she was feeling –

MARY. Yes, I've never done that, either. I can't understand how people live with themselves – blurting it all out – right or wrong, kind or unkind. Expressing themselves, regardless of the damage.

DAVID. It's the new age. The Primacy of Feeling... Feelings above all else. After a while it became rather wearing.

MARY. Mine would never have worked out either.

DAVID. Wouldn't it?

MARY. He played the lute.

They look at each other for a moment. DAVID steps forward. Silence. He takes another step. MARY doesn't move away so he moves close to her. He takes her hands. Finally, after quite a long silence, they kiss. The kissing becomes more passionate. Finally, they break.

For what it's worth... morally speaking... I have never once questioned your stand about these balloons.

DAVID. Haven't you? I have, Mary. Oh, God in heaven, I have. Every single day.

They kiss again and move toward the hall door.

Lights to black.

5.

DAVID *and* LEE *sitting at the table, playing Kerplunk. Later.* DAVID *removes a stick from the stack.*

LEE. Why is there something instead of nothing?

DAVID. God.

LEE. In the universe, I mean.

DAVID. I know what you mean.

LEE. Why is there a universe at all? Why did he make one? What, was he lonely? Bored? And why did he make us – the human race – if all we're going to do is fuck him off?

DAVID. 'Fuck him off'?

LEE. Get on his tits. All he does is moan about us – or send the fucking floods or whatever. Why didn't he just create a race of perfect artificial intelligence that was programmed to do what he wanted, and then sit back and watch the show?

DAVID. I expect he's listening to you right now, and kicking himself.

LEE. Why is there a heaven?

DAVID. Lee –

LEE. Is it a garden?

DAVID. I hope not.

LEE. Why?

DAVID. Because I would prefer it to be a moderately sized city. With a film festival, and a tram system. Possibly a Waitrose.

LEE. They say it's a garden.

DAVID. They say all sorts of things.

LEE. They say it's a big white hall with everybody floating around, singing.

DAVID. Yes, that's the worst-case scenario. Everything white – dry ice… Like a perpetual Westlife concert.

LEE. What do you know about Westlife?

DAVID. I have two daughters.

LEE. One of your daughters thinks I'm scum.

DAVID. You were cruel to her, at school, it seems.

LEE. That wasn't me. I'm not a racist… And anyway, we were only little… I know people who are a lot more racist than me –

DAVID. I try not to look at it in those terms.

LEE. What terms?

DAVID. As something you are. I try to look at racism as something you do.

LEE. Why?

DAVID. Because if it's something you are, then you and it are indivisible. It can't be changed. If it's something you do, you can atone for it. You can say sorry. You can try harder.

LEE. Can I show you something on my phone?

DAVID. Is it another skateboarding accident?

LEE. No.

DAVID. Is it a masturbating gibbon?

LEE. No.

DAVID. Then, yes.

LEE *gets up and goes to his coat to fetch a phone.*

LEE. Here – There was an accident on Jawbones Hill tonight.

DAVID. There was?

LEE. Just before I came here.

DAVID. Who?

LEE. No one. Grockles.

DAVID. Grockles are not no one, Lee.

LEE. Proper smash. Quite nasty.

DAVID. I hope this isn't what you're going to show me.

LEE. No – I'm trying to cheer you up.

DAVID. Cheer me up?

LEE. Another car goes over the edge at Jawbones – that's a good thing for you.

DAVID. What on earth are you talking about?

LEE. It gets you off the hook –

DAVID. Lee –

LEE. I mean it. It proves that that stretch of road is dangerous. That's – When they start to go on at you for writing your car off on Jawbones Hill, you can tell them – it's a fucking deathtrap up there.

DAVID. What else do you know? About the accident? Was an ambulance called?

LEE. Fatalities.

DAVID. No.

LEE. That's what they're saying.

DAVID. Who? Lee, I need to know this – Did Joy Sampson go up there?

LEE. I don't know.

DAVID. Who told you this?

LEE. They were saying it as I came down.

DAVID. Who were?

LEE. People. On their way to the blessing.

DAVID. What people?

LEE. I don't know. I overheard it. I thought you'd be pleased.

   MARY *comes in*.

DAVID. Have you heard about an accident on Jawbones?

MARY. What?

DAVID. Lee says there was another car accident.

MARY. There's always a prang up there. It's a blind spot.

LEE. See? That's what I'm telling him.

MARY. Lee, aren't you going to watch the blessing?

LEE. It's finished now.

MARY. Is Naomi back?

DAVID. Not yet.

MARY. What about Craig?

   DAVID *shakes his head*.

   Where are you staying at the moment, Lee?

LEE. I shift about.

MARY. Yes, but where.

DAVID. You were sleeping so soundly. Why don't you rest?

MARY. If Naomi comes in this way, will you call me?

DAVID. Where's Susannah?

MARY. Wherever Craig is, I expect. Did you hear me, David?
   She's been out all day –

DAVID. She's enjoying herself.

MARY. Call me. Please.

She goes, gesturing to DAVID *as she does, indicating that*
LEE *should go.*

LEE. She wants me to go.

DAVID. Nonsense.

LEE. She sees me as the source of all your troubles.

DAVID. What is it you want to show me?

LEE. How do you feel about being mugged off by the new vicar?

DAVID. I haven't been 'mugged off', whatever that means.

LEE. Yeah, you have. If it was a popularity contest between you
and him –

LEE *puts the phone in front of him. A video plays for a*
second. DAVID *pales, takes the phone.*

DAVID. What the hell is this?

LEE. It's funny, isn't it?

DAVID. It's – Whose car is that?

LEE. Janet Oram's.

DAVID. Lee, what the hell – ? What have you done?

LEE. It's fucking funny, Vicar. It's sick.

DAVID. It's – yes – sick. That's – Sick is exactly – What is that?

LEE. It's cowshit.

DAVID. What?

LEE. I piled it up with cowshit and then set it on fire.

DAVID. Lee, have you any idea what you've done here? How
dangerous it is?

LEE. I took it up to a field. It wasn't dangerous. I thought you,
of all people, would be pleased.

DAVID. Of course I'm not pleased. This is – You've committed
a crime here, Lee. More than one. You've stolen a car.
You've destroyed it. You've started a fire –

LEE. Talk about gratitude.

DAVID. Gratitude?

LEE. You might at least say thank you.

DAVID. Lee. I am going to have to report this.

LEE. What?

DAVID. What choice do I have?

LEE. Oh, that's fucking brilliant that is.

DAVID. You've done something terrible.

LEE. And what about you? You're no fucking better than
    anyone else!

DAVID. Keep your voice down.

LEE. I won't. I won't keep it down. Fuck you.

DAVID. Lee –

LEE. Fuck you. Hanging out with me one minute then being the
    high-and-fucking-mighty vicar the next – I thought we was
    mates.

DAVID. Lee, stop it –

LEE. You wait.

DAVID. Listen –

LEE. You wait. You're a liar and a hypocrite, that's what you
    are. You're a fucking arsehole. You're going down – you
    know that?

    MARY *comes in*.

MARY. What on earth – ?

LEE. You too. Both of you. The whole fucking lot. You're
    hypocrites. Your time is up – yeah? So fuck yourselves. Fuck
    you all.

    He runs out.

MARY. Well, that was an eventful game of Kerplunk.

DAVID. He's a very troubled young man.

MARY. David – when will you see that he is not your responsibility?

DAVID *puts his coat on.*

Where are you going?

DAVID. I can't let him run off like that.

MARY. You're not supposed to leave the house.

The front door slams. Voices.

DAVID. Look. They're back. The whole thing's over.

MARY. That doesn't mean there won't be people on the street – David –

SUSANNAH (*offstage*). Mum?

DAVID *leaves.*

MARY (*calling after*). David – Stay – Please. Stay with me.

SUSANNAH *and* CRAIG *come into the room.*

SUSANNAH. What's going on?

MARY. Your father's gone out.

SUSANNAH. Where?

MARY. Have you seen your sister?

SUSANNAH. No. The blessing went very well.

MARY. All I wanted was just a moment's peace... Just... I'm going upstairs.

She goes. Silence. SUSANNAH *turns to* CRAIG. *Smiles.*

SUSANNAH. Shall we – ? You don't mind if I have a drink, do you?

CRAIG. I'll have a water.

CRAIG *smiles.* SUSANNAH *leaps into life. Fetches bottle, glasses, etc.*

I was worried about that step –

SUSANNAH. You didn't trip –

CRAIG. I would have done. I steadied myself. And the swaying –

SUSANNAH. I told you you'd get used to it.

CRAIG. Do you think my prayers were alright?

SUSANNAH. Oh, completely.

CRAIG. I didn't expect the mic to be quite so close. I felt like Christina Aguilera.

She brings him a water. She has a whisky. They clink glasses.

SUSANNAH. They're going to have you take over... I'm telling you... At least for the time being –

CRAIG. Your father is still officially the vicar.

SUSANNAH. They won't keep him. Not after this.

CRAIG (*uncomfortable*). Susannah –

SUSANNAH. He'll be retired off. They might send him somewhere remote. They might... I don't know... Just send him on his way.

CRAIG. I don't feel very comfortable discussing this –

SUSANNAH. He's made his bed, Craig. Quite literally, as it happens. And I would rather have you stepping into his shoes than some other... (*Beat.*) Is it your partner? Is that the problem?

CRAIG. I don't think he'll come here.

SUSANNAH. Why not?

CRAIG. He wants to get married. (*Beat.*) He wants to get married, and I'm a vicar. How's that for stinging irony?

SUSANNAH (*realising*). Ah.

CRAIG. It isn't the sexuality. That's not an issue. We can live together... We can share this house together... But as long as we're... They consider us to be a 'friendship'. 'A celibate friendship.' Marriage is between a man and a woman. (*Beat.*) He won't put up with that.

SUSANNAH. So what will you do?

CRAIG. I think this is my vocation. What *can* I do?

SUSANNAH. Can I suggest something? I want to help.

CRAIG. You do help. You help me every day.

SUSANNAH. No, but –

CRAIG. Haven't you...? What about you – ? I never hear anything about your life. Men, for example –

SUSANNAH. There aren't any men. Not here. Not the kind of people, I... I can't find anyone.

(*Downs her Scotch.*) I don't stand out. That's the thing. And if you don't stand out, you don't get noticed... I've tried. God knows... But when I look at Naomi – the things she does, the risks she takes...

CRAIG. You *do* stand out. Your deeds –

SUSANNAH. Deeds?

CRAIG. Your actions.

SUSANNAH. Don't patronise me. Please... (*Beat.*) Do you really think there's a God?

CRAIG. I'd be a pretty strange priest –

SUSANNAH. And do you really think he's benevolent? I mean – here's you, with your partner – a cruelly, impossible situation... And here's me... Wanting things I can't have... Can't... *ever* have.

CRAIG (*gesturing at her glass*). Let me have a sniff.

SUSANNAH. No.

CRAIG. A sniff won't kill me. Please. It's good, it stops me thinking about it.

She brings her glass close. He breathes in deeply.
SUSANNAH *watches him. Their faces are very close.*
SUSANNAH *leans in to kiss* CRAIG – *who instinctively recoils slightly.* SUSANNAH *instantly pulls back, mortified.*

SUSANNAH. There. That was a risk.

She moves away.

CRAIG. Susannah –

SUSANNAH. You'll need someone to run this house. That's what I'm saying. Someone like my mother. This parish cannot be run alone. And if your partner... I could help you.

CRAIG. Listen –

SUSANNAH. I don't expect anything. I'm not... You needn't worry about *that*... I just wanted... Just once in my life, to kiss someone I wanted to kiss... It's nothing... And you have my word that it will never happen again.

CRAIG. Susannah, please –

SUSANNAH. My solemn word... Let me help. Let me serve the parish and help you. Please. I haven't much pride, have I? Please... (*Beat.*) A celibate friendship.

Silence. A noise, off. Shouting from outside – it's DAVID.

DAVID (*offstage*). Mary – ?

SUSANNAH goes to the door.

SUSANNAH. Dad?

DAVID (*offstage*). Where's Mary?

DAVID returns with LEE close behind. LEE hovers at the door. MARY appears.

I need the phone.

MARY. What's the matter?

DAVID. It's Naomi.

MARY. What?

DAVID. Where's the phone?

MARY. It's supposed to be in its nest – It's –

DAVID. Please –

SUSANNAH. I'll get it.

MARY. What's happened?

DAVID. I had a text message. Two. From Naomi.

MARY. What did they say?

DAVID. I think she needs help.

MARY. What are you talking about?

DAVID. She sent me a couple of messages –

SUSANNAH. Here –

The phone handed over.

DAVID. There's no signal – the town is full of people, it's always – you can't dial out, you can't send a message –

MARY. What did they say?

DAVID. I'm finding her number...

MARY *waits.*

MARY. Did you see her, Susannah?

SUSANNAH. No.

MARY. Did you?

CRAIG. I didn't see anyone. I mean, apart from the crowd – And she wasn't there. She wasn't at the front.

MARY. What did they say?

DAVID. What?

MARY. The text messages. For God's sake, David –

DAVID. Have you had one?

MARY. I don't know. Have I?

MARY *goes for her phone.* SUSANNAH *too.* DAVID *has the phone to his ear. A moment.*

DAVID. ...Voicemail.

MARY (*looking at phone*). No. Nothing. (*To* DAVID.) You said she needed help.

DAVID. Yes –

MARY. Help?

DAVID. Yes. 'Help.' That's what the first one said – The second one said, 'Help me.'

MARY. 'Help me'?

SUSANNAH. She must have been joking?

MARY. For heaven's sake. Somebody must have seen her. Who are her friends? Who would she call?

LEE. I saw her.

They notice him for the first time.

MARY. Lee?

LEE. I did. I saw her. Sorry –

DAVID. How long have you been standing there?

LEE. Sorry – I thought –

DAVID. When?

LEE. Couple minutes ago.

MARY. Where?

LEE. Has Joy Sampson been up?

DAVID. What?

MARY. No. Where did you see her?

LEE. I thought – I was coming up because I thought she'd have been here.

DAVID. What are you talking about?

MARY. Oh my God.

DAVID. What are you saying, Lee?

SUSANNAH. Why would Joy Sampson be here?

CRAIG. I'm going to call her.

MARY. Yes.

CRAIG. I'll call the station.

SUSANNAH. What's going on?

CRAIG *takes the phone and leaves.*

DAVID. What is it, Lee? Where did you see her?

LEE. I can't. I don't know what to say.

MARY. Just say it.

LEE. I can't.

DAVID. Lee, for God's sake, just spit it out.

LEE. I saw her. (*To* DAVID.) I'm sorry. About the things I said –
About the things I said when I was leaving –

DAVID. It doesn't matter about that.

LEE. I think, perhaps you should wait for Joy –

DAVID. So help me God –

SUSANNAH. It's alright, Lee. Just tell us. Just tell us what you
know.

LEE. She was in the car.

DAVID. What car?

LEE. She was in the car.

Beat.

MARY. Jawbones.

LEE. Yeah.

MARY. She was in the car that crashed.

SUSANNAH. Jesus Christ.

LEE. She was, yeah. Sorry.

SUSANNAH. How is she? Is she hurt?

DAVID. Is she alright?

SUSANNAH. Is she badly hurt, Lee?

MARY. Where did they take her?

LEE. Erm... Torbay, I think.

MARY. I'll get the car.

SUSANNAH. You'll never get out – the roads are jam-packed.

LEE. You will if you go round Totnes way.

MARY. I'll get the car – David, for God's sake get ready –
Susannah, if there's no reply at the station I want you to go
down there –

SUSANNAH. I'm coming to the hospital.

MARY. Do as I ask, Susannah. Please.

They've both gone.

DAVID. Who told you this, Lee?

LEE. I saw her.

DAVID. Yes, you keep saying that.

LEE. Just now. They couldn't get the ambulance out because of
all the cars. They tried to get round Swannaton Road, but…
In the end, they brought her up the back of Above Town, and
I was walking home from here, so – I saw them.

DAVID. Whose car was she in?

LEE. I don't know. Some bloke. She was pretty pissed. She'd
been out all day.

DAVID. You spoke to her?

LEE shakes his head.

You spoke to someone else?

CRAIG appears. Grabs his coat.

Who did you speak to, Lee?

CRAIG. There's no reply at the station. Susannah wants to
come with you to the hospital so I'm going to run round
there. I won't be long. Keep your phone with you, David. I'll
call as soon as I have news.

He goes.

DAVID. Who did you speak to, Lee? How did you see her?

LEE (*covers his face with his hands*). Oh my God…

DAVID. You got into the ambulance?

LEE nods.

This makes no sense.

LEE. Bob Fleet was driving it. They couldn't get past the cars –
People park all up and down when there's a thing on in
town – you know that – they park all over the place. They
were looking for the owner of a blue Saab that was blocking
the way, and, Jill Speake got out, and I... The doors were
open –

DAVID. Lee –

LEE. Vicar, I have to tell you something. I couldn't say it when
the others were here.

A honk from MARY*'s car horn outside.*

She's dead.

Silence.

She's dead. She died. I'm so fucking sorry.

Again – another car horn.

DAVID. What are you talking about?

LEE. I'm sorry. She was bashed up so bad. She was bleeding. Jill
Speake said, 'Stay the fuck out of there, Lee.' I said 'I know
her, alright? That's the vicar's daughter.' She said 'Stand back.'
I said 'That's the vicar's daughter, that's Naomi Highland.' And
she said. 'Was.' (*Beat.*) 'Was the vicar's daughter.'

DAVID. What?

LEE. That's what she said. She's a fucking arsehole, Jill
Speake – She hates me, she always has –

DAVID. Lee –

LEE. And I could see. I could. That's why they went the other
way, you see? The other way to the hospital. Wasn't so
urgent. Otherwise they'd move the traffic, wouldn't they?
Put the sirens on. I'm sorry, Vicar. I'm so sorry.

MARY *comes in.*

MARY. We need to leave.

LEE. Mrs Highland, I'm so sorry.

MARY. What? What's going on?

DAVID. Don't say anything, Lee. Don't say a word.

MARY. What? What is it?

DAVID. It's nothing.

LEE. It's not nothing.

DAVID. Go back to the car, I'll be right out.

LEE. She's dead, Mrs Highland. She died.

MARY. What?

LEE. I'm so sorry.

MARY. What are you talking about? What do you mean?

DAVID. Lee has a theory.

LEE. It's not a theory.

DAVID. He thinks he saw something.

LEE. I did see something.

DAVID. Lee, I want you to go now.

MARY. What? What did you see?

LEE. I saw her in the ambulance –

MARY. No –

LEE. I saw her in the ambulance and Jill Speake said she was
    bashed up so bad she was dead.

   MARY *stumbles*. DAVID *rushes toward her. She pushes him
   away, presses her hand over her mouth and stifles a huge
   guttural cry. A noise from the depths – but suffocated by her
   hand.*

   SUSANNAH *comes in.*

SUSANNAH. What's happened?

DAVID. You're lying, Lee.

LEE. I'm not lying.

DAVID. Admit that you're lying.

LEE. I'm not. I'm fucking not. She's dead alright? Fuck off.

SUSANNAH. What happened? What is he talking about?

MARY. Oh Christ... Oh Jesus Christ...

SUSANNAH. Oh my God – What? Is she dead?

DAVID. Mary –

SUSANNAH. How? How can she be dead?

DAVID. I want you to tell me the truth, Lee –

LEE. I swear to you.

DAVID. Hasn't anybody got through to the police station? Where is the phone? For God's sake –

LEE. I swear I'm telling the truth. I saw her –

DAVID (*screams*). Jesus Christ, where is the fucking telephone, for fuck's sake!

DAVID screams in frustration and rage – And then crumples. Little silence.

LEE. I saw her. I saw her through the windows. I saw her face. I saw her hands all covered in blood. I saw the expression on her face. I saw her eyes open and they weren't moving – I saw her.

MARY. Oh God –

LEE. And I thought to myself – Well, now they'll know how it feels.

Silence.

DAVID. What?

LEE. Now they know how it feels to lose their little girl.

Beat.

DAVID. What did you say?

LEE. Now they know what it feels like.

A little silence. LEE *stretches out his arm, points his finger, and very slowly and mirthlessly laughs at* DAVID *like a child in a playground.*

Ha. Ha. Ha.

A little silence. NAOMI *appears at the open door behind* LEE.

NAOMI. I'm having a shower. I just lost my phone at The Floating Bridge and I'm covered in cider. Jesus, this town is unbearable –

She walks out and into the house. Both MARY *and* SUSANNAH *stagger from the shock.*

SUSANNAH (*quietly*). Jesus Christ…

MARY. Naomi –

MARY *rushes after her.*

Naomi – ?

She's gone.

SUSANNAH. You sick little fuck.

DAVID. Leave us alone, Susannah.

SUSANNAH. I'm calling the police. Fuck you. You'll suffer for that.

DAVID. Go.

SUSANNAH. You're an animal. An animal.

She goes. Beat.

LEE. There's her phone.

He tosses it into the middle of the room.

I didn't send the messages. That was two girls. They found her phone at the pub and they thought they'd give you a taste of your own medicine. I just…

DAVID. What?

LEE. I just took it to the obvious extreme.

Silence.

DAVID. You must be very pleased with yourself.

LEE. Wait till I tell Tina.

DAVID. Yes. Go. Go and tell Tina.

LEE backs off toward the door.

LEE. Now you know. Now you know the feeling.

He goes. DAVID collapses onto a chair. Silence. Some incoherent shouting from offstage.

DAVID. Naomi?

More shouting, then silence. CRAIG appears.

CRAIG. Apparently Joy Sampson is on her way up here.

DAVID. Yes, we know.

CRAIG. There was an accident apparently, but of course they wouldn't confirm or deny –

DAVID. It's fine. She's here.

CRAIG. What?

DAVID. She's here. She's upstairs.

CRAIG. Oh, thank God.

DAVID. Yes. It was a case of mistaken identity.

He weeps. CRAIG takes him in his arms for a moment.

CRAIG. Thank God.

DAVID moves away, pulls himself together. SUSANNAH comes in.

SUSANNAH. Jesus. Are you alright?

DAVID. Yes.

SUSANNAH looks at CRAIG. He nods. It's fine.

CRAIG. I'll –

DAVID. Thank you, Craig.

SUSANNAH. Yes. Thank you.

CRAIG. If you need me –

DAVID. Thank you, Craig. Thank you very much.

He leaves. A little silence.

What's going on out there?

SUSANNAH. She's losing her mind about her phone.

DAVID. It's there.

NAOMI (*offstage*). Susannah!

SUSANNAH takes the phone and goes back in. Silence. DAVID sits. JOY appears at the door. She watches for a moment then knocks on the frame.

JOY. Vicar?

Nothing.

We need you.

Her walkie-talkie bursts into momentary life.

I'm sorry, Vicar –

DAVID. What?

JOY. We need you.

DAVID. Who needs me?

JOY. Road traffic accident. Jawbones Hill. They've taken them to Torbay but the gentleman who was driving seems to be on the way out… Visitors.

Silence. DAVID comes round somewhat.

DAVID. Ah.

JOY. They've asked for a priest. The wife has, anyway. We don't know if they're Catholics or what – there's a little crucifix thingy hanging from the rear-view mirror… I can give you an escort…

DAVID. Alright.

JOY. I'll be outside.

> DAVID *nods. In a rather dazed state, he searches for his coat and his car keys.* MARY *comes on.*

DAVID. I have to go to the accident... The real accident.

MARY. I wished it was you.

> *Silence.*

DAVID. Mary –

MARY. That's what I thought. I wished it was you that was killed – That's what I thought when he said it.

DAVID. I expect I'll be late.

MARY (*quietly*). Christ in heaven, show us mercy. Christ... In heaven...

> DAVID *puts on his coat and leaves.* MARY *is left alone.*

> *Lights fade to black.*

6.

Bright morning. CRAIG *and* JOY. JOY *has a mug of tea.* CRAIG *is a bit restless.*

JOY. It's strange. Apart from David, I'm not often alone with a priest... Sort of a weird sensation, isn't it?

CRAIG. Is it?

JOY (*quickly*). Not that, I'm – I'm not saying you're going to molest me, or anything.

CRAIG. I'm... Just for the avoidance of doubt, Joy – absolutely *not* going to molest you.

JOY. That's the spirit. (*Beat.*) It's all got to stop anyway, hasn't it? All this molesting. I don't just mean you lot in the church. It's everywhere... Offices... The Olympics... (*Beat.*) Old

Ted Goddard – the other day – said he'd been the subject of unwelcome advances in the workplace. I said – 'How the hell does that work, Ted, in your line of business?'

CRAIG. What does he do?

JOY. He's our gravedigger.

CRAIG *takes that in.*

You're not doing the funeral, are you?

CRAIG. No.

JOY. I think it's going to be a pretty big number.

CRAIG. They've got the choir.

JOY. They've got the lot. Bigger than the river blessing, people are saying. They've sold out of balloons at Argos... I've heard of people going to Dawlish to get them.

CRAIG. What are people going to do with all these balloons?

JOY. I don't know... I think they're all going to let them go at some point. So they can... You know... float up to heaven or whatever... (*Beat.*) Nice, really... Only, apparently they're quite bad for the seagulls.

CRAIG. Do you think there'll be trouble, Joy?

JOY. My presence is largely symbolic. A deterrent. I just hope I don't go into labour...

CRAIG. That's not very likely, is it?

JOY. You never know. I wet myself in hot yoga last week...

She puts her tea on the table, walks over to the window, peers out.

One or two of the Evangelicals was asking about power points. So they could play their guitars.

CRAIG. They can't. Anyway, the organ will be going full blast.

JOY. That's what I told them. It's not sodding Glastonbury. They give me the creeps, if I'm honest. Why do they have to smile all the time? I suppose you've spotted their new recruit –

CRAIG. Yes.

JOY. He's got a brass neck banging a tambourine with a court date hanging over him.

CRAIG. 'There is more happiness in heaven over one sinner who repents...'

JOY. Not Lee Southbury. They'll be locking the doors and windows. If I was Jesus – which, obviously, I'm not – I'd be like – 'No way, Lee. I'm all for the odd sinner here and there, but that doesn't mean you can take the piss.'

Beat. She appraises him for a second.

Must all be starting to feel a bit real now.

CRAIG. What?

JOY. You taking over.

CRAIG. I haven't... That's not necessarily what I'm going to do.

JOY. Frightened, are you?

CRAIG. Frightened?

JOY. That you might end up back on the piss.

CRAIG. What on earth makes you say that?

JOY. I've got an antenna for these sorts of things. It's the blessing and the curse of my work. Human nature. I suppose that's something we've got in common.

MARY *comes in. Dressed for the funeral.*

MARY. Isn't he back?

CRAIG. Not yet.

MARY. I want to be prepared in case of emergencies. Craig – If, by any chance, he can't go on –

CRAIG. Do you think that's possible?

MARY. Anything's possible. He could be booed off. He could be jeered at –

CRAIG. But surely not at a funeral –

MARY. The days when this was purely about a funeral have long passed. I want you to go into the vestry and robe up. A simple cassock will do. Just in case you have to step in.

CRAIG. Alright.

MARY. I don't think it'll happen, but if it does – Have you seen Susannah?

CRAIG. She's getting ready.

MARY. I think she should carry the cross. I think if we go out family first, we'll show that we're not afraid. I think that's the thing – don't you? A show of solidarity.

CRAIG *nods. Leaves.*

A final show of solidarity.

JOY. It's true then, is it, Mary? You're going.

MARY. I'm going somewhere, yes.

JOY. Away from the town?

MARY. I shouldn't think so. I think it would be very strange to abandon the town after all this time... I have been offered one of the charity flats.

JOY. At Norton House?

MARY. Exactly. I can't decide whether it's appropriate to take alms from a committee I once sat on... or completely inappropriate...

JOY. You could go back to your maiden name.

MARY. I could.

JOY. Mary Norton of Norton House. Sounds posh.

MARY. Yes, doesn't it *sound* it.

Beat.

JOY. Hard, isn't it? Life.

MARY. It is, Joy. It is hard.

JOY. Clint's always relentlessly cheerful – I can never understand it. I see the world for what it is after sixteen years in the force... I'm always anxious. All the time. Funny, isn't it?

MARY. That's not a word I would have associated with you.

JOY. I cover it up. I think you need to get on with things, really.

MARY. Quite right. That's the spirit.

JOY. I do worry about having another miscarriage. If I'm honest. I've never... I've never carried one this far before... So that worries me.

MARY. You're going to do just fine, Joy.

JOY. Thank you, Mary. That means a lot...

JANET pokes her head in. She's wearing a huge, oversized T-shirt.

JANET. Oh. Sorry. I just – they're asking about barriers, Joy –

JOY. There's the tape we use for the fun run. They can use that.

JANET. Will you please come and tell them? It's an absolute nightmare out here.

JOY. I'm coming... Anyone would think Justin Bieber was on his way... I'll be back in a minute to escort the coffin, Mary.

MARY. Thank you, Joy.

She goes. JANET stays. MARY busies herself. Beat.

JANET. Mary –

MARY. I see you've got your T-shirt.

JANET. Oh, don't. Please. It's ridiculous... They wanted one size to fit everyone, and... Well, I mean look at it... I've told Peter – his number-one priority after this, has got to be some kind of healthy-eating programme up on that estate. It's a scandal. And, of course, I can't take it off now –

MARY. No. You can't.

MARY works on.

JANET. I must say David's letter was very impressive.

MARY. Letter?

JANET. About my car. I'm preparing my victim statement. He made a very emotional case for clemency –

MARY *works on, no answer.*

He's more to be pitied, isn't he? Lee Southbury? And David was very... He can be very convincing, can't he? About forgiveness?

MARY. It's a very convincing idea.

JANET *shrugs, nods.*

JANET. I don't know why you judge me.

MARY. I beg your pardon.

JANET. Oh let's be real for a minute. I know what people think of me. It's funny – I always used to excel at everything I did. Honestly. But here... I don't know... This may be a funny moment to say this, Mary, but – I wish I knew you better.

MARY *looks at her. Silence.*

I think we've covered a lot of the same ground. I know how it feels to be... Waiting around for Peter to come home. Not knowing where he was. Or... rather... Knowing *exactly* where he was. I do know how that feels.

Silence.

I just... If you ever wanted a coffee –

MARY. Thank you.

JANET. Or a chat –

MARY. I'll bear that in mind. Will you excuse me?

MARY *leaves the room – into the house. JANET reflects on how poorly that went. Turns and examines herself in the mirror again. Then – a thought strikes her. She takes the excess fabric of the T-shirt and ties it in a side knot – like a beach garment – immediately making it fit closer to her body. She regards this in the mirror, smiles. MARY returns. JANET is slightly busted.*

JANET. I just… I'll see you in church…

> DAVID *walks into the kitchen. A moment as they look at each other, then* JANET *leaves, flustered.*

DAVID. Where's Craig?

MARY. He's robing.

DAVID. What for?

MARY. Because I told him to. I think we'd better have a standby… Anyway – if the worst comes to the worst – he can assist.

DAVID. We're not doing communion.

MARY. He can stand there and look pretty. What does it matter? I want you supported.

> *Beat.*

DAVID. My hands are shaky.

> *Silence. They look at each other.* MARY *walks to the cupboard.*

MARY. I suppose if you limit yourself to just one.

DAVID. Do you think it's wise?

MARY. Well, if you can't get through it without… Can you?

> DAVID *shakes his head.*

DAVID. You do the measure, will you?

> *She takes out a bottle of Scotch and pours him a glass. She brings it over.*

MARY. Sip it.

DAVID. They'll be able to smell it on my breath.

MARY. Well, they can't fire you twice, can they?

> *Beat. He takes it. Sips it and puts it down on the table.* LEE *appears at the door.*

LEE (*subdued*). Morning, Mary.

MARY. Lee. Are you staying with the Evangelicals or are you coming in with the family?

LEE. I've got every right to come in with the family.

MARY. I didn't say you didn't. I only asked.

LEE. I am. I'm coming in.

MARY. Very well. I'll go and check on the bollards. We may need some kind of crowd control by the sound of it.

She leaves. Beat.

LEE. There's a lot of my lot out there.

DAVID. Yes, I believe so.

LEE. I say 'my lot', they're not... They don't mean any trouble. They're backing me.

DAVID. Good.

LEE. Supporting me... I've flourished in the love and support of Jesus Christ over the past couple days. I've grown in it. That's what Keiran says.

DAVID. I'm glad to hear it.

LEE. I'm not saying I'm one of them. I'm only... I'm only saying... It's clarity. That's Keiran's watchword. The Divine Light Mission is clear. There's no doubt. Only the certainty of being saved –

DAVID. That must be very comforting.

LEE. It is. I don't know why you don't try it.

DAVID. I don't try it because life isn't like that. It's nuanced. You, of all people, should understand that, Lee. It's a mess.

JOY comes in.

JOY. I've spoken to your mum, Lee. I think it's probably better that you stay with your born-again lot this morning.

DAVID. He's sitting with the family.

JOY. I'm not sure that's wise, to be honest.

LEE. I can sit wherever I like.

JOY. Today is about Taylor, Lee. Not you. And I think you'll be interested to know that the two girls who found Naomi's phone –

DAVID. I don't want to hear about that.

JOY. They've confessed to everything. They say you egged them on.

LEE. I didn't.

JOY. They say they wanted to give the phone straight back.

DAVID. I told you, Joy, I don't want to hear about that. Not today.

CRAIG *comes in*.

CRAIG. Susannah's asking for you, David.

DAVID. Thank you. I take it you'll be in the church?

JOY. Outside. The only thing I'm worried about is crowd control. I'm not sure we're going to get all the cars through.

DAVID *leaves*.

Where's Mary?

CRAIG. I'm afraid I don't know.

JOY *leaves*.

Lee, you'd better get moving if you're joining your friends from the Mission.

LEE. I'm not. I'm going with the family... You want to come up there some time, Vicar. See how it's done.

CRAIG. I'm sure I will.

LEE. You better prepare yourself though. It's zero tolerance for gays up there.

CRAIG. Lee, if you'll excuse me – I have to find my stole.

LEE. Keiran would forgive you... He would forgive you – But he'd tell you he cannot walk beside you – That's – Not without condemnation of your lifestyle.

CRAIG. Right.

LEE. That would be his message to you. Forgiveness but not acceptance. His love is abundant, but he follows the word.

CRAIG. Believe me, I know the type.

He's gone. MARY *enters.*

MARY. You're going to follow the coffin, Lee? You're sure.

LEE. Why does everyone keep asking me that?

MARY. Well, you'd better go and find your family. We'll be walking in very soon. Go and find Tina and tell her to come in here – and the rest of them – as many as are following.

LEE. Alright –

MARY. But family only, Lee.

He goes. NAOMI *comes in. She looks chastened. Quieter.*

NAOMI. I'm going home after this.

MARY. Are you? That's a shame.

NAOMI. I've got an audition.

MARY. Oh – ?

NAOMI. What can I say? I'm a show pony. I get it from Dad. (*Beat.*) I want to say something.

MARY. You don't have to –

NAOMI. I want to. (*Beat.*) You know why you didn't get a text, don't you – ? When I was… When you thought I was hurt… You're in my phone as 'Mother' – That's the thing I want you to know –

MARY. You don't need to explain anything to me –

NAOMI. But she's in my phone as 'Mum'. That's – That's why she got it and not you.

A little silence.

MARY. She *is* your mum.

NAOMI *nods.* DAVID *comes in.*

DAVID. I think we'd better start moving.

MARY. Naomi's going back to London straight after.

DAVID. Oh.

NAOMI. I was explaining about my mum... My...

MARY. I told her there was nothing to explain.

NAOMI. No, but...

DAVID. We're delighted that you found her.

NAOMI. I still come from here.

MARY. Of course you do.

DAVID. Is she well? I always hoped to meet her myself.

> NAOMI *is suddenly overwhelmed with feeling. After a silence –*

NAOMI. She's been through a lot.

> MARY *goes and hugs her. Silence.*

DAVID. I'll pray for her.

MARY. I pray for her every year. I put flowers in the Lady Chapel and I light a candle. I do it on your birthday. I think that must be the hardest day.

DAVID. Naomi, Lee Southbury is going to be back in a minute.

NAOMI. It's okay.

MARY. It's a day when we're all going to have to bite our tongues.

NAOMI. It's fine. I'll be fine... I believe he's 'seen the light'.

MARY. Let's go and get ourselves ready, shall we? Give our faces a wash...

> *They exit, crossing* CRAIG.

CRAIG. Sorry – have you seen Susannah?

DAVID. In the vestry.

CRAIG. David – when this is over – can I speak to you? As a priest –

DAVID. I won't be a priest when this is over –

CRAIG. As a friend then. Please. I'm drowning – I'm really struggling –

TINA *arrives at the door.* CRAIG *leaves.* TINA *walks in. She has no balloons.* DAVID *sees her, they face each other for a moment.*

DAVID. Are you alright, Tina?

TINA. I take one breath. One step. And I think... Right... Now another one.

DAVID. One at a time... You're not on your own?

TINA. I don't want to stand out there. I don't... Got anything to drink?

DAVID *looks around for his glass of Scotch. Hands it to her.*

Silly question in here. (*Takes a sip. Hands it back.*) Doesn't work on me no more. Drink. I used to love a bit of... I used to... But now...

DAVID. Come in. Come in and sit down.

TINA. Got my fucking balloons, didn't I?

DAVID. You did.

TINA. Got my five minutes of fame.

DAVID. I hope you know – I hope you understand that it wasn't personal. It was never intended to hurt you.

TINA. How could it hurt me? How could anything hurt me?

TINA *reaches into her bag. She pulls out a piece of paper.*

These fuckers all standing outside holding balloons – they don't give a toss about Taylor. Or me. Or anything else. When all this is over – by the end of the day, to be honest – they'll all have fucked off. What'll I have? A load of rubbish. (*Beat.*) I'm sorry you had to lose your job and your house and that.

DAVID. Yes. Well. Thank you.

Silence. She offers the paper to DAVID.

What's this?

TINA. It's a picture Taylor did. It's the river. That's... I told her her dad worked on the ferry. He didn't, actually, but... Anyway, she was a good artist. She liked drawing... I thought you'd like it because of... I don't know... The sky. She's done all the different colours in the sky. All the rays of the sun. It's sort of... You know... Heaven, or whatever.

DAVID. I think it may be the most beautiful thing I've ever received.

Silence. MARY *comes in.*

MARY. David –

Silence.

They can't get the hearse up because of all the people.

DAVID *pulls himself away from the picture.*

DAVID. What – ?

MARY. The hearse.

DAVID. Are they bringing her in here?

MARY. Is that alright?

DAVID *looks at* TINA.

DAVID. Sometimes... it happened when the wall outside collapsed last summer –

TINA. What?

DAVID. We can't bring the hearse to the west door... It's nothing to worry about.

TINA. What does it mean?

DAVID. It means we bring the coffin in through this way, and process out of the door and round in to the church. Will that be alright?

TINA (*stricken*). I don't know.

MARY. We don't really have much choice I'm afraid, Tina.

JOY. We could take the long way, start the procession early.

MARY. How will Mr Pearson know when to begin?

SUSANNAH *comes in.*

SUSANNAH. Are we bringing the coffin through here?

DAVID. Just wait, Susannah.

SUSANNAH. I'm sorry, they just – They want to know –

DAVID (*to* TINA). Take your time.

TINA *looks to* DAVID, *panicking.*

TINA. What do you think?

DAVID. I think we should bring her in here. We've done it before.

MARY. We did it with my father, in fact.

DAVID. Let's have her with us, then we can all be together.

TINA. Okay.

DAVID *looks at the others. They nod.* JOY *goes.*

I don't know how I'm going to do this.

DAVID. Take deep breaths. There's nothing that can happen that you will have to bear alone. The whole town is here. We are all bearing you up. Together.

LEE *comes in,* CRAIG *and* NAOMI *and* SUSANNAH *are with him.*

TINA. What's going to happen?

DAVID. When they bring Taylor in here, what we'll do is – we will take a little moment. I'll say some prayers. First for Taylor – then for us. Then we'll carry her into the church –

TINA. My mum's waiting outside.

MARY. Would you like me to fetch her?

TINA. No. She can – It's… I can just…

DAVID. We can scoop her into the procession as we go. That's not a problem.

TINA. Right.

DAVID. Everything is going to be alright. I will be beside you throughout.

TINA. Yes.

DAVID. Okay?

TINA *nods*.

Are you ready?

TINA. I don't know.

DAVID *holds out his hand. She takes it. She breathes. He looks at* MARY, *who nods and exits.*

LEE. This is unbearable. I can't do this. I can't.

The coffin comes in through the inside door. It's very small, and carried by just one or two PALLBEARERS. *At the sight of it,* TINA *crumbles.*

TINA. Oh God –

DAVID. It's alright.

TINA. I can't – Oh God – I can't. Oh no. Oh no.

DAVID *very gently leads her to the coffin and stands in front of it.*

DAVID (*quickly and plainly*). I am the resurrection and the life, saith the Lord: he that believeth in me, though he were dead, yet shall he live: and whosoever liveth and believeth in me shall never die. We brought nothing into this world, and it is certain we can carry nothing out. The Lord gave, and the Lord taketh away; blessed be the name of the Lord.

MARY/SUSANNAH/NAOMI/CRAIG. Amen.

DAVID *stands, staring at the coffin for a moment, then –*

DAVID. Save me, O God, for the waters are come in, even unto my soul. I stick fast in the mire, where no ground is, I am come into deep waters, so that the floods run over me.

I am weary of crying, my throat is dry, my sight faileth me for waiting so long upon my God...

Deliver me out of the mire, and let me not sink: let me be delivered from them that hate me, and out of the deep waters.

LEE (*distressed*). Tina –

DAVID. Hear me, O God, in the multitude of thy mercy, even in the truth of thy salvation. Take me out of the mire, that I sink not; O let me be delivered from despair, and out of the deep waters.

LEE. Tina, you've got to forgive me –

MARY (*soothing him*). Not now, Lee. Not now.

She guides him to a chair where he slumps.

DAVID. Let not the water-flood drown me, neither let the deep swallow me up, and let not the pit shut her mouth upon me... Let... Let not...

He grinds to a halt. A moment. MARY *quietly speaks –*

MARY. Hear me –

DAVID. Hear me, O Lord for thy loving-kindness is comfortable; turn thee unto me according to the multitude of thy mercies. And hide not thy face from thy servant...

He stops again.

I – I'm sorry, I –

MARY. For I am in trouble.

DAVID. For I am in trouble: O haste thee, and hear me. Draw nigh unto my soul, and save it; O deliver me, because of mine enemies.

Silence. The coffin is borne up and they start to process out. DAVID *continues to intone the Psalm. The organ can be heard from the church. We hear the gathered people outside singing: 'All People That on Earth Do Dwell'.*

LEE. You've got to forgive me, Tina. You've got to.

The procession moves out. SUSANNAH *leading with the cross, then the others. Soon, they've all gone. Only* LEE *remains.*

You've got to forgive me... Please. You've got to forgive me.

Finally LEE *leaves. The room is empty. Only the thundering of the organ, and the singing.*

The End.

www.nickhernbooks.co.uk

facebook.com/nickhernbooks

twitter.com/nickhernbooks